ENGLISH
MISERICORDS

HIDDEN beneath the tip-up seats in the choir stalls of many English churches and cathedrals are some of the most vivid images that have come down to us from the Middle Ages. Their originality of design, breadth of subject-matter and artistry render these misericords England's finest surviving mediaeval wood carvings. These sculptures were normally out of sight, so the craftsmen felt free to carve everyday scenes and animals from their own lives as well as the monsters and mermaids that swarmed in their imagination, rather than the religious subjects one might expect.

With recent advances in photography Marshall Laird has been able to capture these misericords, ill lit and awkwardly positioned as they are, in this beautiful pictorial survey. In addition to an Introduction explaining their development and the sources and meanings of their imagery, he has written a valuable appendix on how the amateur photographer can tackle them with ease. This book opens up a whole new area of study in English churches, a possible successor to brass rubbing.

DR MARSHALL LAIRD has spent his life in the field of vector pathology. He was first drawn to mediaeval misericords by the quantity of flora and fauna they depicted. He has recently been appointed an Honorary Research Fellow at the University of Auckland in his native New Zealand.

ENGLISH MISERICORDS

MARSHALL LAIRD

JOHN MURRAY

The bird monster supporters on the half-title
page are from Lincoln and the sun on the
title page from Ripple, Worcs.

First published 1986
by John Murray (Publishers) Ltd
50 Albemarle Street, London W1X 4BD

Printed in Great Britain
by BAS Printers, Over Wallop, Hampshire

British Library CIP data
Laird, M.
English misericords.
1. Misericords—England   2. Choir-stalls—England
3. Wood-carving–England   4. Cathedrals—England
I. Title
729′.93   NK9743
ISBN 0-7195-4268-5

CONTENTS

INTRODUCTION

MISERICORDS are carved corbels, topped by a narrow ledge for half-sitting against when vertically positioned, on the underside of tip-up seats in the choir stalls of mediaeval churches. They are fashioned from the same (usually oaken) block as the pivoted seat itself. Their originality of design, breadth of subject-matter and artistry render them England's finest surviving mediaeval wood carvings.

In the primitive Christian church all stood to pray. Even when kneeling was adopted for part of divine service, the old and infirm were disadvantaged. This was particularly so among the monks of enclosed communities, singing, chanting and intoning in the choir, where, by the 10th century, rows of seatless stalls (from Old Teutonic and Anglo-Saxon words for 'standing') began to appear. 'Before very long,' seats, 'in the form of brackets, which worked on pivots,'[12]* were being introduced into these stalls. However, they were only to be turned down and sat upon during 'the Epistle and Gradual at Mass and the Response at Vespers.'[6] By the 11th century, although the sterner disciplinarians were deprecating sitting in church at all, reform was in the air. In 1121 the Cluniac Benedictine, Abbot Peter the Venerable, became the first to record the existence of *scabella*, small sitting places attached to the seats as an indulgence. These were now mentioned as 'misericords' at the German Monastery of Hirsau. They clearly solved the problem of taking the weight off one's feet better than the earlier device of *reclinatoria*, or leaning staffs.

The Latin word *misericordia* means 'pity' or 'mercy'. While in this instance a relaxation of the Benedictine Rule was conveyed, the term also referred to other kindnesses; ranging from provision of a special dining place for clerics with dietary problems, to the daggers used for the *coup de grâce*. All other names for choir stall underseat ledges such as 'nodding stools',[37] 'baberies'[12] or 'misereres',[6] are incorrect.

The need for the misericord did not outlast the Reformation. Nowadays the name particularly applies not to its purpose but to its decoration; the carving of the corbel and undersurface of the tip-up seat itself. Supplemen-

*Superior figures refer to the References to be found on p. 127, those in brackets to the Plates.

One of the seats in the choir stalls at St George's Chapel, Windsor, tipped up to display the misericord.

The leaning staff in use. This was a forerunner of the misericord (New College, Oxford).

tary, or wing, carvings, termed 'supporters', are a primarily British innovation. In continental Europe, the great majority of misericords consist of an unsupported centrepiece. Although the 3400 or so remaining in the United Kingdom and Eire are considerably less than half the number of those surviving in France,[35] the fact that most have two supplementary carvings besides that of the corbel gives them the largest number of subjects in what from the standpoints of originality, workmanship and interest is the finest regional collection of all.

In the first century from the start of the Gothic building boom, eighty cathedrals and some five hundred abbeys were built in France alone.[51] 'Kervers' were quick to appreciate the possibilities of decorating the under-seat ledges of so many new choirs. In monasteries of enclosed communities these were inaccessible to the laity, and the choir was also generally screened off from the public in parish churches and cathedrals served by monks, canons or secular priests. Moreover, being turned downwards when not in use, misericords were not on constant display. Here, then, was a place where apprentices learning their craft could try their skill. It was also one where the expert carver could freely indulge his imagination and sense of humour, qualities shared by the sculptors ornamenting stone-work high on the columns and walls and otherwise out of close public view—notably roof bosses[11] that gained in altitude as Gothic evolved.

A central bracket supports the oval-fronted underseat ledge of the few remaining early 13th-century misericords. The best—Exeter Cathedral's—were heavy-handedly 'restored' in 1870.[12] There the ledge tapers into the flat undersurface of the tip-up seat. At either end is an embryonic supporter, and the medial strut is lightly ornamented (63). Twenty years later a centrepiece dominates the misericord, the supporters now being carried outwards and downwards from the ends of the ledge on moulded connectors (52). The presumably primordial stage, altogether unornamented (not to be confused with much later unadorned misericords like those of St Nicholas, Swineshead, Beds), is absent from Exeter or anywhere else. Did the simplest form prevail in the lost choirs of 12th-century Cistercian abbeys (p. 14), where it is said that aside from the stylised 'water leaf' motif of stone capitals[8] figural art was eschewed?

The only remnant of the 13th-century set discarded from Westminster Abbey in about 1509 serves as prototype for most future misericords, its underseat ledge topping a swelling corbel (122). Deepening and thickening, the ledge improved perching prospects for the plumper clerics. It gained more support from the sturdier corbel, and became shaped and moulded in ways offering stylistic clues to the dating.[6] Sometimes it was even decorated, the most attractive examples being at Lincoln where tiny roses embellish the face of the ledge (29, 104, 113, 143). The 1305 supporters at Winchester Cathedral (102, 103), carried well out onto the board on scrolled bead mouldings, are most unusual in dwarfing the centrepieces. This trend climaxes at Lavenham, Suffolk (59), where the central carving almost disappears. Conversely, Gloucester Cathedral's mid 14th-century misericords have their centrepieces framed not by supporters but by exuberant cusped foliar decoration across the whole board (8, 71, 125). Better than any set elsewhere, they 'disguise the indulgent purpose of the ledge' and 'reflect the medieval allergy to a bare surface'.[35]

Supporters, although present in eighty percent of British misericords and their outstanding national characteristics, are not peculiar to Britain. In France, for example, besides scattered 'misericords with added features at the sides', about one-third of Albi Cathedral's have wing carvings.[22,35] It would have been less confusing had the latter term always been used, for 'supporters' has an allied meaning in heraldry. There it describes the figures on either side of a shield, often holding it up. In their free-standing form on ancient tombs these were allegedly derived from the seal-engravers' solution to 'filling the awkward space between the shield and the margin of a round seal.'[1] In their turn the misericord-carvers, 'by giving a bolder curve to the moulding and greater importance to the supporters . . . achieved a perfect balance of carved and plain surfaces'[2] (105). Brother craftsmen in stone and wood must each have applied their solutions to the decoration of circular roof bosses,[11] which, like many misericord supporters and the medallions of Romanesque wall paintings and Gothic stained glass, may have had their genesis in manuscript illuminators' roundels; in their turn evolved from Islamic and Byzantine textiles and ivories, characterised by heraldic animal designs of Sumerian origin.[34]

Only about two percent of the supporters of English misericords have the same design as, or a similar one to, that of the centrepiece, or are known to interact with the latter. Beverley Minster is particularly rich in examples of close similarity between all three designs.[58] New examples of interaction in this book include the heron of the centrepiece and related leg-rings of the supporters at Herne (55).

When classifying subject matter, problems soon arise. Misericords that are sharp satires on mendicant friars are common in churches once under Benedictine control. Thus the cape and knotted cord belt of the Franciscans are worn by the fox-friar preaching to geese at Etchingham (98). Is this to be classified under 'humans', 'animals' or 'religion'? Again, many subjects to which mediaeval people would have responded with alacrity, are incomprehensible to modern viewers. Similarly, we may still be amused by a century-old humorous cartoon, while finding its original caption boring or pointless. How much harder, then, to bridge social and cultural gaps of several centuries.

Most misericord compositions are secular. Their analysis for multiple meanings, a subtlety dear to medieval minds, is rewarding. While certain themes and individual subjects recur, in some cases frequently, there was clearly much freedom of choice about what was carved. There has been great destruction of church woodwork over the years, some of it selective. Initially, therefore, the proportional representation of major subjects might have been very different from today's. Nevertheless, the latter is of interest.

Crudely carved Janus-headed wyvern, between unique vertical supporters in the form of head-downward snakes (Weston-in-Gordano).

Thus only about 4.5 per cent of Britain's almost 8,600 surviving centrepieces and supporters have primarily religious significance, and 1.5 per cent are Scriptural, as compared with over twice that in France. However, the figure becomes comparable with Britain's if just two cathedrals (Amiens with 110 Old Testament subjects and Auxerre with 41 New Testament ones[35]) are omitted. One explanation for so low an incidence of religious topics at the very heart of churches is that some 'clerics were delicate about allowing the lower body to be in contact with the effigies of Christ, Mary, or the Apostles'.[35] Another is the eagerness of the carvers to exploit the potential of a usually hidden location.

Rather more than 4,000 (about 48 percent) of British misericord centrepieces and supporters (particularly the latter) include plant subjects. These range from stylised foliage through naturalistic fronds, flowers, fruits and seeds to material derived from herbals and the *Physiologus* (p. 18). There are also conventionalised trees, foliate masks and even cloves in the Arms of the Grocers' Company. Next to botanical subjects in order of abundance come animal ones, amounting to about 24 per cent of the whole. There are mammals, birds, reptiles, amphibians, fish and a few invertebrates, not to mention borrowings from one or more of these valid groups for the hybrid horde of monsters, many of which have a dash of humanity as well.

Some of the attempts to portray foreign fauna were less successful than others (71, 72). However, Matthew Paris[38] left us a presentable drawing of an African elephant, St Louis' gift to King Henry III. This marvel of the day was seen by multitudes on its 1255 plod from Sandwich, Kent, to London, and there at the Tower until its death four years later. Whether having himself viewed the animal over the heads of a crowd (for he got the feet wrong) or through access to the Matthew Paris drawing or a copy, the carver of the Exeter misericords produced at this stage a perfectly recognisable representation of the African elephant. All its successors are the smaller-eared, howdah-bearing Indian species (80), drawing on the Bestiary tradition, in so far as they are recognisable at all. As to British wildlife, a few species were naturalistically shown on misericords over the next four centuries, sometimes even with a suggestion of the appropriate ecological background (55, 63, 123).

Humans themselves, from the highest to the lowest, with their homes, hopes, fears, quarrels, ailments, pleasures, tales and sayings, are third in line as proportional subjects (about 18 percent of the total). Heraldry accounts for about 3 percent. The remaining 2.5 percent is made up of subjects bridging different groups of living beings, humanoid monsters in particular.

The ingredients for a rebirth of Western Culture in the 11th century were a diminution of fears about the imminent end of the world, the spread of a new social framework in the form of feudalism, and—thanks to better agricultural practices—improving nutrition. That heralded Last Day at the start of the year 1000 had dawned and anticlimactically died like any other, and the small beginnings of questioning and doubt are there to be discovered in the welter of figures exuberantly carved by stone-masons living in the challenging aftermath. Thus here and there, tongue-in-cheek details leaven the awful inevitability of all the great Last Judgements of Romanesque cathedral portals. The less-than-terrifying demon above the lintel of the West Door of Ste Foy de Conques seems to be remarking 'Good luck!' over his shoulder to a similarly half-turning soul behind him—just on the right side of centrefield, and clearly surprised at finding himself there. These figures, and still more so the nubile Eve of Autun Cathedral, would have been quite beyond the conception of Carolingian craftsmen. So would the charming little rabbits of the corbel-table at Kilpeck, Hereford-shire, mid 12th century.

By the early 1100s the huge new Romanesque abbey of Cluny was the largest Western church. Its monks could no longer journey abroad building fresh churches themselves, as in the heady days of the First Crusade. Divine service, with up to 138 psalms to be chanted during the daily offices,[42] was now to occupy most of their time. This brought dire need for relief from interminable standing and kneeling unsupported. Thus at the very time when Cluny's Abbot Peter signalled the arrival of that relief via misericords, anonymous lay workers were of necessity assuming the major role in church construction and decoration.

In England, as Norman influence strengthened, the stone ornamentation of churches displayed Signs of the Zodiac, animals of the Bestiaries, satires on strolling players, chevron markings and monsters. Notable among the latter were Nordic beak-heads, oddly neglected by the misericord-carvers. Otherwise, as summarised in the next section, these made enthusiastic use of the rest of the stonework motifs. Soon after Early Gothic reached England in the mid 1170s, the national variant, 'Early English' emerged. A leading characteristic was stiff leaf trefoil ('stiff' from its stylised stems rather than the leaves). For a while this dominated stone capitals, but after the mid 13th century such conventionalised work yielded to naturalism in the transitional period to 'Geometric Decorated'. By the 1290s the new development matured into the astonishingly beautiful leaves and flowers embellishing the capitals of Southwell Minster's Chapter House.[50]

The longer 'Curvilinear' phase of the Decorated endured through the first three-quarters of the 14th century, characterised by its continuous double (ogee) curve. The form of the misericord was now diversifying. Semi-oval ledges with quite shallow mouldings had lasted through the 1200s (114, 122). The resting surface became centrally hollowed (19) and thus somewhat more comfortable. By the mid 14th century it was often frontally straight (8). By the end of Decorated architecture the ledge was sometimes four- or six-sided and variously scalloped or straight-edged, with a central point in front (124). Rising to the challenges thereby presented, the carvers diversified their subject matter. They were to achieve their masterpieces in the century forever remembered for the Black Death of 1348–49.

Lay woodcarvers, their homes or lodgings scattered among the general population, struck better odds for survival than monks packing enclosed communities or masons crowded in their lodges. Infection in the great plague pandemic, whether pneumonic or flea-transmitted, was favoured by congestion. Even in isolated monasteries there were terrible losses. Thus at Meaux, Yorkshire, only ten of fifty brethren survived.[16] Such casualties were central to the eclipse of English manuscript illumination,[34] while comparable mortalities among masons ended individualistic Decorated achievement. The ensuing drastic shortage of stone-carving skills led to shopwork which, as the Perpendicular style developed, eventually filled some of the niches with statuary carved elsewhere but left others forever untenanted.[26] Their different life-style and the fact that they were less bound by precedent led to the misericord carvers (and embroiderers) keeping alive the imaginative tradition of figural representation after the Black Death until the end of the Middle Ages.[34]

Even so, twelve of Wells' sixty-four misericords were never completed. While these carvings are said to have been made by ca 1340, it was not unusual for such work to proceed slowly—at Exeter Cathedral, for example, it had been spread over nearly fifty years. Work may well have been proceeding on some at the plague visitation, the death of a key craftsman leaving his carvings unfinished. Again, at Gloucester the southern misericords date from ca 1340; but the northern ones were not completed until about 1360.[23] These vigorous and innovative carvings, like those of late 14th-century Worcester Cathedral, exhibit an unusual number of Scriptural subjects. Could this reflect renewed personal preoccupation with things religious among those carvers still active after a pandemic that killed more than a quarter of England's population?

Across the Channel, the progress of church construction and decoration was impeded by not only the Black Death, but also the Hundred Years' War. The quality of French misericords carved during these years lagged accordingly.[35] Accelerated by the contract-work imposed by the Black Death, however, England's Perpendicular style was flourishing towards the end of the 14th century. By then a recovering France had for once followed an English architectural lead, by importing the previous Curvilinear Decorated style and verticalising the ogee curve to initiate its own Flamboyant period. The distinctive Perpendicular endured throughout 15th-century England, when the form of the underseat ledges was altering again. By the middle 1400s a thick bracket, capping a corbel carved in shallow relief around three facets, was common (28). Plant naturalism now reverted to conventionalised though often sophisticated decoration. Underseat ledges continued to thicken and became ever more complex in their horizontal grooving (20, 30, 46, 73). By 1520 Beverley Minster had the front of the by-then otherwise ungainly ledge enriched by a row of mini-arches between horizontal groovings (5).

When all but one (122) of Westminster's 13th-century misericords were discarded in about 1509, the new carvings of the stalls of Henry VII's

Chapel brought a foretaste of the Renaissance. One, which could hardly have come from any other than an Italian hand, shows a decidedly post-Gothic Wodehouse family disporting naked among grapes. Elsewhere, still-exuberant Gothicism persisted into the 1520s at Bristol Cathedral and Beverley Minster. Soon afterwards, the great days of an essentially mediaeval art form ended not with a whimper but a gratifying bang in the splendidly original subjects at King's College Chapel, Cambridge (109, 118). Pure Renaissance work, these were carved in the very decade of Henry VIII's destruction of the monasticism that had posed the need for misericords in the first place. And as a pointer to England's mercantile future, arms granted to the Grocers' Company on the eve of the Dissolution were duly added to earlier misericords at Cley, Norfolk.[15]

By March 1540[40] the last of the great monasteries had fallen. What *had* survived the pillaging, unroofing and torching of the King's servants amounted to perhaps 10 percent of 'the most wonderful woodwork the world has ever seen'.[30] Gone, for example, were the choirs of towering 12th-century Cistercian abbeys. Fountains and Rievaulx (N Yorks), Furness (Cumbria), Netley (Hants) and others were now but sorry shells. Over and above their presumably strictly functional misericords there must have been innumerable carved examples at Glastonbury (Somerset) and other desolated Benedictine monasteries. The Cluniac love of elaborate liturgy expressed in the rich decoration of their cloister arcades and other surviving stonework renders it likely that there was marvellous woodwork in their thirty-two priories and single abbey, at Bermondsey. All were destroyed, as were many houses of other Orders.

Prominent among the surviving churches were great ones that had been served by Canons Regular. In priests' orders and living in cloistered communities, these had given the laity access to their churches and sometimes conducted parish services too. Other ancient foundations weathered the storm because they had been served by Canons Secular. Also in priests' orders, each of these had dwelt in his own house. Colleges of Canons Secular had been attached to parish churches with choir stalls (and therefore misericords) to serve chantry chapels built in the 14th and 15th centuries. The authority of Canons Secular was now extended to cathedrals from which Benedictine monks had been ejected, including Ely, Norwich and Winchester. And the former Austin Canons' church at Bristol was elevated to cathedral status, as were the lately Benedictine houses of Chester and Gloucester.[8]

Woodcarver, his apprentices at work behind him and his dog at his feet. The supporters show (left) a saw and the initial 'U' and (right) a gouge or chisel like that being used by the carver, and the initial 'V' (Victoria & Albert Museum).

Many stalls in these and other churches were left unscathed. Others were not, their misericords being defaced or destroyed. Thus the popular St Thomas à Becket, all figures of whom were outlawed in 1538 by Henry VIII,[1] survives in only one misericord, long hidden and later built into the lectern at Fornham, Suffolk.[2]

Misericords were at length carved again. At Wimborne in Dorset, after the spire collapsed, carving covered the entire underseat, beneath heavy ledges, with lightly stylised foliar and fruit decoration (1608). A decade later, restoration began at Cartmel Priory, where twenty-five salvaged misericords dating back two hundred years were positioned in new stalls beneath a fresh Renaissance canopy. Among other such moves, new misericords were made at Brancepeth, Co Durham, in 1626–33. The wealthy and dynamic John Cosin, fired by visions of an imminent return to ancient liturgies, was then Rector there. Despite the support he enjoyed from King Charles I and the future Archbishop Laud, he played it safe; all the carvings, like the contemporary ones of Lincoln College Chapel, Oxford, were discreetly floral. Later Master of Peterhouse, Cambridge, he was ejected from office for spiriting away the Plate to the Royal Mint at York.[20] Cosin passed the Civil War and Protectorate in Paris. Returning at the Restoration, he saw to the carving of England's last 'real' misericords in Co Durham. Defiantly Gothic, their subjects ranged from heraldry to Durham Cathedral's men, monsters, plants, birds, lions and squirrels—as well as the only crabs to figure on British misericords. This fitting Indian summer of the art, replacing what Cromwell's Scottish prisoners had destroyed while incarcerated in the Cathedral, was the handiwork of not only the last of the pure line of English misericord carvers, but also the only one whose name is almost certain: James Clement of Durham.[48]

From early in the 18th century onwards, additional misericords (collectively called 'modern') were carved at times. Thus at, for example, Arundel Castle, Henry VII's Chapel at Westminster, and St John's College Chapel, Cambridge, many such examples have reproduced or replaced decayed earlier ones.

Not all damage to English misericords was on the grand scale of the Reformation. Wood-boring insects and dry rot did their share from early times, and continue to do so. Puritan iconoclasts destroyed many precious things, but their activities were concentrated upon the more visible woodwork of screens and canopies. Even when they did turn their attention to misericords, they sometimes did not go beyond the cutting away of crucifixes and other parts of subjects involving the Virgin and saintly martyrs. Greater acts of vandalism were committed by 19th-century prudes. Dean Howson, for example, expunged five of forty-nine late 14th-century misericords that he found 'very improper' in Chester Cathedral.[48] And during a 'restoration' at St Nicholas, King's Lynn, a carpenter was told to burn the stallwork he'd been required to remove. Thanks to his own views on the matter, several important misericords (see p. 15) came into the possession of London's Victoria & Albert Museum. However, in a book published as recently as 1932, G. Long could still state that 'even since I have been studying church carvings, some of the cruder and more objectionable misereres have been removed or censored'.[37] More innocently, ancient misericords 'cut and hacked by generations of schoolboys' are exhibited in the Library of Henry VIII's Grammar School at Coventry.[48] And an intermittently out-of-action tongue wags within the lips of a 1305 hooded head centrepiece at Winchester Cathedral.[37]

Losses among the eighty-nine churches burnt in the Great Fire of London, 1666, must have been incalculable. In the case of Old St Paul's Cathedral, there is a tradition that misericords now at Bishop's Stortford (54) were taken there from its remains.[46] All but two of York Minster's late 15th-century examples were burnt when a lunatic set fire to the choir in 1829. Britain's only set of misericords illustrating the Dance of Death, a subject otherwise shown only by one Windsor example (12), was lost

The Woodcarver in close-up.

with the rest of St Michael's Cathedral and much of Coventry by Nazi air attack. A decade afterwards fire destroyed nine late 15th-century foliar carvings at St Michael, Tettenhall, Staffs, and while this was being written York Minster's conflagration of 1984 threatened those two surviving misericords which had been placed in the Zouch Chapel after the 1829 disaster. However, during the blaze 'Two of the clergy did in fact heave the stalls out into the open air . . .'[54] The Chapel was untouched and its misericords are back in place.

In a summary of the sources from which carvers drew inspiration, first and foremost comes the evidence of their own eyes. From the outset, they copied stiff leaf and other foliar designs (52), Signs of the Zodiac, animals and monsters from stonework in churches where they worshipped and worked. It has been suggested[30] that the deep undercutting of early miseri-

17

cords at Exeter (100) betrays the actual hand of the stone-mason.

Doubtless, too, friendships were struck up between wood-carvers and monks. The latter, while working at copying tasks or studying, must sometimes have been impressed by the suitability as a model for a particular misericord subject that had been discussed, of a marginal illustration; itself perhaps derived from figured silk, carved ivory, or some other Eastern souvenir bargained for or looted during the Crusades or afterwards imported as business prospered. A cleric would probably have been as reluctant to bring a precious manuscript to the work-site as to invite a somewhat grubby craftsman to the library. However, dashing off a sketch and handing it over would have meant little trouble to him while stimulating his carving acquaintance to tackle, say, one of the popular topsy-turvy themes such as a pig musician (78, 79) or a hare riding a hound (89). A century or two earlier the stone ornamentation of Canterbury Cathedral had so originated,[60] and the route would have been equally likely for misericords. Moreover, verbal descriptions alone might often have served this purpose in a day when a strong oral tradition and very retentive memories offset illiteracy.

Another source of ideas for misericord subjects would have been the earlier Continental experience of immigrant craftsmen. Flemish workers were much sought after for their outstanding carving skills in mediaeval times. It has been claimed that recruiters lured them to England by extolling the 'good beer, soft beds, and pretty girls' to be had there.[35] Such men would have certainly seen Romanesque carvings and perhaps manuscript illustrations too, portraying the fanciful 'Plinian races',[24] a mixture of travellers' tales and misinterpreted fact gathered together by Pliny[29] from earlier Latin and Greek authors, and further embellished for eventual mediaeval credulity in the dawn years of Christianity by 'the *Physiologus*'.

This shadowy figure from the Alexandrian world in its transition from latest Antiquity to earliest Christian times, gathered an assemblage of fact intermingled with folklore going back through Pliny and Ancient Egyptian sacred symbolism[17] to long before the time when the first horsemen sweeping down into northern Greece were rationalised as centaurs. By the 12th century few Western monasteries could have lacked a manuscript version of the works of the *Physiologus* ('Natural Philosopher') as processed through Alexandrian hermeneutics and even (in the 6th century) denounced as heretical.[17] In classical and several vernacular renderings the book had become *the* clerical guide to pseudoscience.

18

Moralising tales told from the *Physiologus* must have been as familiar in mediaeval ears as Bible teaching. An 11th-century version[49] long served as a schoolbook in the later Middle Ages. By then 'Bestiaries' were even more widely available. These were illustrated derivatives and transmutations of the *Physiologus*. They blended (often wildly misinterpreted) observations of animal characteristics and behaviour with much misinformation and allegory, designed for the chief purpose of representing all creatures great and small as existing solely to reveal some aspect of God's will. Examples common on misericords are the Pelican in her Piety (p. 31, No. 71) and the Mobbed Owl (66). Manuscript Bestiaries were adorned with marginal illuminations confirming textual errors and adding more of their own. For example, animals from mammals to insects were commonly shown as three-toed. Dutifully transferred to misericords (51, 52) this distinctive feature is a sure morphological marker of a Bestiary source. Was there a reference to the Holy Trinity here, as in the case of Romanesque trefoils? By the second half of the 15th century printed versions of the earlier manuscripts and encyclopaedic texts based upon them, were being marketed—sometimes, as in early printed herbals, the same woodcut was made to serve for more than one subject. Such texts included *De Proprietatibus Rerum*,[53] *Hortus Sanitatis*[31] and Albertus Magnus' *The Book of Secrets*. As an example, an English version of the second, *The Noble Lyfe & Natures of Man . . .* appeared about 1521 complete with many 15th-century woodcuts showing a diversity of actual and imaginary beasts, still sporting those three toes. Even as the Middle Ages were dying, craftsmen with increased access to literature could thus find in the latest books authority for carving such divorced-from-reality symbols as the Pelican in her Piety. Despite their capacity for achieving natural likenesses, they would doubtless have gone on following such Bestiary precedents even had they themselves seen the utterly different natural pelican and its nest.

Legends, romances and folktales were always rich sources of inspiration for misericord-makers. These included the 12th-century ones of the *Chevalier au Cygne* (p. 27, No. 25) and *Tristan and Iseult* (p. 28, No. 26). A French romance of the same period led to several representations of the trapping of Sir Yvain (from the early 14th-century English translation, *Ywain and Gawain*) (23). A folktale not printed for another three-and-a-half centuries, *Jack and the Beanstalk*, has key incidents from it carved at New College Chapel, Oxford, late 14th century (117). Other familiar tales including versions of the Beast-epic of Reynard the Fox were likely to be heard whenever jongleurs were entertaining. However, Reynard's adventures are mainly presented after their transformation 'into didactic allegories'.[56] Bristol's sequence (94, 95, 96, 97), although sometimes claimed to be derived from William Caxton's *The History of Reynard the Fox*, 1481,[48] embody features suggesting an earlier French source despite their late date.[56]

When naturalistic carving emerged at the Early English/Decorated transition (52), carvers of wood and stone both now had models for fashionable leaf decoration to hand from the nearest trees. At the workplace, other waiting subjects ranged from the cat and its latest mouse to bats (with satisfyingly devilish features, moreover!) sometimes found dead on the church floor. The 14th-century bats at the cathedrals of Wells and Hereford (76) are so naturalistic that their carvers must surely have been working from freshly dead specimens. Yet, so powerful were the effects of Bestiary misinformation and so much was and is observation conditioned by the accepted *schema*, that the tremendously lengthened fingers supporting the membranous wings were grossly misrepresented. Of course, such a matter must have seemed as trifling as the usual three-toed state of the Bestiary fauna, to one as innocent of anatomical niceties as a man of the Middle Ages. In the mid 16th century, Hans Holbein's Dance of Death skeletons were still anatomical disasters.

The Bible inspired specifically religious misericords indirectly as well as directly. Thus now-vanished Romanesque murals were the sources of some.[14] Again, morality plays were familiar to mediaeval townsfolk, including the mobile wood-carvers responsible for Ludlow's Dishonest Ale-Wife and Hell-mouth (99) and the several versions of chatterers in church (110) whose gossip was recorded by the demon Tutivillus. For the former's downfall featured in the Chester Mysteries (played annually within about sixty miles of Ludlow); and Tutivillus starred in the Wakefield (Towneley) Doom Play.[3] Far older performances of pagan origin were still to be witnessed too. These included seasonal mummery concerning the Ages of Man (2), the Occupations of the Months (4), the Feast of Fools and similar cyclical events. By the Wars of the Roses the blooms of both persuasions were being carved, as were other emblems such as Warwick's Bear and Ragged Staff (133). The climax of misericord-as-Media was reached with the depiction of the Peace of Picquigny (p. 28, Nos. 30, 31, 32), arranged by Edward IV on 29 August 1475 near Amiens with Louis XI of France. By the end of the century a craftsman found it prudent to portray himself on a Great

Doddington (Northants) centrepiece carving the new Tudor Rose and flanked by others as supporters. News was travelling faster, and so was printed material. Earlier in that last decade of the 1400s the first English misericords definitely established as having been modelled on pictures in a printed book, were carved at Ripon Minster. Comprising four Scriptural subjects (141, 142, 144), they were copied not from a book printed with movable type, but the block-book, *Biblia Pauperum*.[47]

The courtly love of the earlier legends and romances is mocked in Westminster Abbey's 1509 Battle of the Sexes scene (20) with its Freudian overtones. This is derived from the ancient tale of the Humiliation of Hercules, and is very reminiscent of French and Belgian misericords where husband and wife fight for the breeches. The wife is seen donning them one-handed in a carving at Hoogstraten while threatening her husband with the inevitable distaff as he dismally winds a ball of yarn onto a frame. This is the selfsame subject of an engraving of 1480 by the Fleming, Van Meckenem.[6] The date would fit nicely with the subsequent arrival in London of some Flemish carver to help in the decoration of Westminster Abbey's Chapel of Henry VII, where Flemings are known to have worked.[7] Perhaps the same man also brought with him copies of the Dürer and Van Meckenem prints which were [4,47] the sources for seven Abbey misericords (15, 16, 17, 18).

Late 15-century editions of the *Travels* of Sir John Mandeville included woodcuts of humanoid monsters to be expected in foreign lands—Blemyae and related subjects of travellers' tales going back to some of the same Plinian races as already mentioned. The artists who designed the blocks for the early editions were as likely to have been stimulated by Romanesque and early Gothic stone-carving as their misericord-carving contemporaries. However, in a 1484 edition[41] is a bat-faced Devil (74), who so resembles Christchurch Priory's 1515 bat as to strain arguments for coincidence. Another popular book of the period was *Le Compost et Kalendrier des Bergiers*.[28] Published in Paris in 1493 this circulated woodcuts of the Occupations of the Months and related Zodiacal and Ages-of-Man subjects already familiar from manuscript Shepherds' Calendars, *Livres d'Heures* and Psalters.[18] There were printed English versions from 1503. The availability of this publication might help to explain the revival of interest in Occupations-of-the-Months scenes in the early 1500s, specific examples being the man-with-assistant in the pig-butchering misericords at Bristol (6) and Beverley Minster, both of ca 1520. Remnant[48] has illustrated a badly damaged centrepiece of ca 1520 from St Michael and All Angels, Throwley (Kent) showing what appears to have been an ape riding a reined monster, alongside the reproduction of a marginal ornament in a printed book whence it was derived. A version of the ape rider, different from but better preserved than the Throwley one, is also present at Bristol, another design from which (107) has its Throwley version too. Both subjects have been shown[14] to be copied from marginal ornaments (108) used by three Parisian printers in the opening years of the 16th century, and afterwards much borrowed.

A really exhaustive study would inevitably turn up other such sequences. However, because of the predilection of early printers for using particularly appreciated woodcuts over and over again and from one publisher and country to another, there is always likely to be a measure of speculation over the precise source of a particular carving. This is, after all, as it should be. For speculation has been and will necessarily remain inseparable from the interpretation of misericords. As printing gathered momentum in other directions it was of course a major force in precipitating the Reformation and in England, the Dissolution of the monasteries.

It was fitting that the end came suddenly. After all, the gulf between the mediaeval tradition (still being pursued at Bristol Cathedral, for example, in 1520) and what would have followed had there been no Dissolution, is immense. The Italianate influences evident at Westminster Abbey and King's College Chapel, Cambridge (109, 118) would clearly have ushered in an entirely new era. In this the bizarre, judging from those King's College monsters, might well have flourished for a while. But with the arrival of the Age of Discovery dragons and unicorns were already endangered species, and the Renaissance had better things in store for plants and animals than a role in outmoded moralising; nothing less, in fact, than their impassioned study as an end in itself as modern science shook free of ancient restraints. Had misericord carving continued in the new spirit, all that could have resulted in England was what actually did happen in France; immensely capable decorative work of a School, rather than the often highly individual efforts of the mediaeval carvers. As things stand, the few 'genuine' Renaissance misericords of England look more in place among the modern, non-functional examples, than at the tail of the Gothic diversity that they had so obviously outgrown.

HUMANS

Seasons of Life and Occupations of the Months

THE SIMPLEST subdivision of human life equated childhood, youth, manhood and old age with the seasons of the year. There are also divisions into seven, ten and twelve. At Sherborne Abbey a mid 15th-century centrepiece (2) shows 'a boy holding a bow and riding an elaborately draped hobby-horse'.[48] The boy is scampering away, his own feet hidden by the flowing drapery of the Hobby. At lower front left the leg seen in the stirrup isn't his. If it was, he would be falling onto his back. It is a stuffed substitute, part and parcel of some hobby-horses of the mumming kind. The arrow slanting down behind the boy's shoulder could either be the last toy one in his quiver, or another that's been shot at him. This particular representation could well combine the 'January' of the Ages of Man with an incident from a local New Year masque surviving from pagan days. Yet another interpretation of this is that it portrays the 'Rider on the White Horse', one of the Four Horsemen of the Apocalypse from Chapter 6 of *Revelations*: 'and he that sat on him had a bow; and a crown was given unto him'. The figure certainly has some sort of circlet on his head. The adjacent misericord at Sherborne Abbey shows a book-clutching boy bare-bottomed over the knee of a birching teacher. This is certainly February in the Ages of Man sequence.[18] A number of misericords have been lost from Sherborne. One of them is known to have portrayed a 'Hunter blowing his horn; dexter, the stag; sinister, the hounds'.[48] This was often the 'March' item of the twelve-picture set on the Ages of Man. Such stag-hunters, their March/Springtime of young manhood previously overlooked, are also carved on misericords at Ely, Bristol, Chester, Gloucester, Norwich and Manchester, as well as at St Mary, Nantwich, St Botolph's, Boston, New College Chapel, Oxford, and several other churches.[48] Twice—at Norwich Cathedral and St Botolph's, Boston—the February theme of the thrashed schoolboy is present as well. It also occurs at Westminster Abbey.

Gloucester Cathedral's 'March' stag-hunting scene is one of two misericords there that may well illustrate Ages of Man. The second is the famous

'Footballers'[6] (8), where the round ball is obviously being bounced by hand, probably by children, representing January. The man and woman seated by a fire (10) from Ripple, represents either December or February. The woman is spinning, the fire does not appear to be lit (suggesting a fuel shortage?) and the man, who perhaps has just brought in the unlit faggots beneath the cauldron, is wearing his hood and two-fingered gloves. There are many problems when it comes to putting in order misericords thought to represent Occupations of the Months. For a start, their original sequence in the choir stalls has usually been completely upset. Calendar changes complicated things and some of the carved representations stem from basically classical themes concerning rather warmer lands than England. There are the usual problems of interpretation too. A misericord at Ripple has long been labelled 'hedging' (February) but probably shows the building of a hovel for 'pease' storage (June).[55]

June's symbol is frequently mowing. Three scythe-wielding men comprise the centrepiece of a ca 1397 Worcester Cathedral misericord; part of one of them, his hands on the grips, can be seen in No. 89. August's predominant motif is unarguable. At Ripple as elsewhere in England, this was harvest time. The couple in No. 3 seem to be reaping a fine head-high wheat crop. They are using the reaping hook or sickle in one hand, and a forked holding stick in the other. Interestingly, the man is left-handed. Judging from the scar at the end of her arm, his wife's reaping hook has been broken away. The subject of No. 4 from the Victoria & Albert Museum (presumably East Anglian and formerly assumed to be from St Nicholas, King's Lynn[48]) shows corn sheaves being forked up to the loader on a cart. Its supporters are of great interest. Previously, they have been taken for bird-headed monsters.[48] It is now submitted that they are in fact mummers, wearing bird masks still echoing pagan times in the late 15th century. The great bustard is the only possible thick- as well as long-necked bird, with a massive head and beak, to have served as the model for such masks. As to why this species should have been associated with harvest-time, Moffett wrote nearly 400 years ago that 'In the Summer, towards the ripening of corn, I have seen half a dozen of them lie in a Wheat-field fattening themselves (as a Deer will doe) with ease and eating . . .'[43] The mummers apear to be mimicking the gobbling of grain left by the harvesters. Perhaps their lineal descendants were the 'Hallering Largess' East Anglian field labourers who were still in the 1890s gathering before their employers' houses after the harvest, forming hand-holding rings, bowing 'their heads very low towards the centre of the circle, and (giving) utterance to a low deep mutter, saying "Hoo-Hoo-Hoo"; then they jerk their heads backwards and utter a shrill shriek of "Ah! Ah!" repeated several times'.[21] The latter would fit with the alarm call of the great bustard, and the former with the 'occasional gruff bark' of the male.[45]

Beverley Minster's proverbial 'cart before the horse' centrepiece (5)[58,48] seems likely to have had an overlooked 'August' meaning, for the earliest of all reaping machines was a cart into which grain was tossed from a front-end cutting or tearing device as a horse pushed it into the standing crop.[25] Threshing (120) and the bagging of corn for malting as seen at Ripple were 'September' motifs. So was boar-hunting (28)—England's last true wild boar survived until 1676.[19] Personifying evil, this beast also symbolised sensual greed.

In October, as in May, the noble sport of hawking was practiced. At Lincoln an especially fine hawking supporter (1) shows a lady with a falcon correctly on her gloved left wrist, a spaniel at her side and eager for the chase. Dame Juliana Berners, 1486,[5] specifies a Merlyon for a lady. This bird, though, is proportionately so much larger than a merlin, that it was probably meant for the other bird of the late 14th-century aristocratic female hawking set: a peregrine falcon.[10] In October, too, a common motif is of pigs being fattened on acorns (49). In France, the picking and pressing of grapes commonly serves for this month. English versions of the vintage, as at Gloucester cathedral (125), have at times been assumed to be merely Continental borrowings via either manuscript illumination or imported craftsmen. However, today's English vineyards remind us how much wine was made here in the past. November pig-butchering is shown in a Bristol Cathedral misericord (6). The remaining activities illustrated in this section are not specifically linked with months. From his clothing, though, the protective shepherd of No. 7 clearly has a wintertime problem. While his salad-bowl hat and blunt-toed shoes suggest the end of the 15th century, the accepted period of the Winchester College carvings to which he belongs is a century earlier. The essential conservatism of country attire must be taken into consideration here. Moreover, the stylish pointed shoes of the 1390s would hardly have suited wintry hillsides. One of the supporters is described[48] as showing a shepherd seized by a lion. It in fact shows a heavily clothed shepherd slipping, perhaps in snow, while bringing in a ram on his shoulder, one gloved hand around its body.

On indoor activities, the tapster from Ludlow (9) is far from nodding off as has been implied.[48] He appears to be operating a spring-loaded flow-control device with his left foot on the treadle, while concentrating on drawing the proper measure from the barrel and thereby avoiding the fate of the Dishonest Ale-Wife (99) across the aisle. Another tavern scene (11) illustrates why backgammon or 'tables' had been proscribed as prejudicial to religion, work and good order.

Also at Windsor is England's only remaining misericord illustrating the Dance of Death. The centrepiece shows Death taking the rich man, and the supporters, his calls on a thresher and a gardener (12). Carved in 1477–83, they probably reflect the major outbreak of plague in 1478–79, one of the great epidemics with high mortality that had been recurring at intervals since the arrival of the Black Death in 1348. Just five years previously an outbreak, which touched the Royal Household, had begun with the sudden death of labourers harvesting near London.[16] In the unusually hot autumn of 1473 other diseases including malaria and dysentery were rife too, and these deaths in the fields must have made a particularly frightening impression.

Men versus Women

As on the Continent, a frequent theme of English misericords was the Battle of the Sexes (p. 21, No. 20). Tenderness is generally lacking, the stolen kiss bestowed by a viol-player on a dancer (Chichester Cathedral, ca 1330) being about as close as the carvers come to such a sentiment (19). And this does not not approach the grace and reciprocity of the young lovers in a Cologne Cathedral misericord of the same century.[35] Did the horrors and mortality of the Black Death and subsequent eruptions of plague and other diseases help to trigger the curious obsession with nudity in Henry VII's Chapel misericords at Westminster Abbey and several of those at Bristol Cathedral (45, 46, 94, 107)? There's a little of this at St George's Chapel, Windsor, too; which for reasons already stated can be linked with severe contemporary disease mortality.

In the light of present-day concern about wife-beating, it is refreshing to note that in fifteen examples of domestic brawls pictured in English misericords, the wife is invariably the aggressor and victor. Moreover, only one of the multitude of misericord women wears a scold's bridle (at Ludlow), and a mere two or perhaps three others (at Durham Castle,

Beverley Minster and Ripon) are on their way by wheelbarrow to the ducking-stool. As recently as 1932[37] the Judith and Holofernes carving at Lincoln (143) was mistaken for a case of husband-beating rather than the biblical scene of the Jewish heroine about to behead the military leader of the Assyrians. Sexual overtones of role reversal and birching are also present, though the 'world turned upside down' or 'topsy turvy' motif (20) is really what was being portrayed.

Kings, Knights, Romances

The late 14th-century illustration of jousting (21) at Worcester Cathedral was one of several copied in a 19th-century restoration at Gloucester Cathedral. There, devoid of much of the immediacy of the original (especially as expressed by the anguished face of the tumbling naker-beater), it shows how such attempts in profoundly different periods and cultures fall short of the original. An interesting detail in original and copy is the notch at the right-top of the shields where the lance was couched in the charge. The butt of the loser's broken lance is still notched, the hand grasping it trapped by the shield driven back against his chest.

A portcullis as seen raised in No. 22 has crashed down in No. 23, trapping the (unseen) hero of Yvain and Gawain who had been pursuing the fleeing knight whose prisoner he now became. The subsequent popularity of the English metrical version as told and re-told by minstrels is evident from the featuring of this particular incident on misericords not only at Chester (1390) but also in three other late 14th-century collections at Boston, Lincoln and New College Chapel, Oxford (where it appears twice). In all cases the same dramatic scene is shown and the two men-at-arms who took Sir Yvain prisoner glare as supporters or from the castle. The story still held enough interest a century later to be re-told at St Mary, Enville (Staffs). In this last, one of the knight's spurs is highlighted (it was to be shorn away by the portcullis); and peering from a window is the damsel who duly showed him the door—literally, for she revealed the postern by which he escaped.

Embodying a design defect which made it especially vulnerable to being sliced through with a blow from a heavy sword or battleaxe, the flat-topped helmet seen in No. 25 enjoyed (like many of its wearers) rather a short life in the 13th century. The story of the Swan Knight is dauntingly complex.[57] It includes Anglo-Saxon, Scandinavian and Longobardian elements which surfaced in ancient Irish mythology and the Arthurian legends before becoming Gallicised under the name of *Chevalier au Cygne*. This hero's praises were sung in mid 12th-century *chansons de geste* by *jongleurs*, half a century before Wolfram von Eschenbach renamed him Loherangrin (afterwards contracted to Lohengrin). Like *Cupid and Psyche* the original tale has to do with the fatal curiosity and inexorable punishment of a lady determined to discover the identity of her unknown lover.

Tristan and Iseult, or Tristram and Isoude, are part of the Arthurian cycle. Going on and on and on, the tale must have been a sort of *Dallas* for 14th-century listeners. The present scene (26) from Chester Cathedral (1390) shows Tristan simply holding hands with Iseult under a tree, through the branches of which his uncle King Mark (Iseult's husband) looks on.[2]

With a tiger cub in the crook of his arm the knight in No. 24 is lying back in the saddle so as to minimise the chance of breaking the mirror he is casting down to divert the attention of a tigress (27) in hot pursuit. This is in accordance with Bestiary advice to the hunter so pursued after stealing cubs, the idea being that the mother would be deluded by her reflection into trying 'to deliver her children out of the glass'[53] thereby allowing the thief time to escape with her litter.

The finest of all representations of a knight in English misericords is Lincoln's luckless one (29). Its carver has caught the very instant of total loss of control as the rider, transfixed by a crossbow bolt that's entered through the unprotected area at the back of his coat-armour, slumps forward over his twisting, collapsing steed. His pointed basinet and riveted camail are typical of the late 14th century. The contemporary use of a ring-mail hauberk beneath plated armour, the arrangements for securing which are said to be an unusually clear representation,[2] is shown almost photographically. A particularly admirable feature is the carving in the round, the craftsman even having managed to work *behind* the rider's head, modelling the visor closed for battle over the averted face.

No misericord comes closer to the reporting of a contemporary news event than does that of the Sovereign's Stall at St George's Chapel, Windsor (30). This was carved somewhere between two years and a decade after the event it depicts, the meeting on 29 August 1475 of England's Edward IV and France's Louis XI to discuss peace terms. The event took place on a bridge, spanning the River Somme, which had a barrier across its centre 'couered with boords ouer head to auoid the raine' and fitted with 'a grate made ouer-thwart with barres, no wider asunder than a man might well thrust in his Arme'.[52] As shown in No. 30 the French party has filed in from the left. One little knight is armed with a great battleaxe almost his own height, and the foremost dignitary, with a hand on the carved post, is probably John, Duke of Bourbon. The figure purporting to be Louis (the head broken away) is stretching his left arm towards the grille. This too is badly damaged, and on its other side Edward's right arm is missing. Distrust was obviously much in the air. Indeed, it is said that Louis' Chamberlain was actually impersonating him 'to reduce the danger of his sovereign being murdered.'[32] Clearly, the 'imbracements' that took place through the grille are imminent. Edward, 'apparelled all in cloth of gold', is crowned. The Royal heaume, likewise crowned, is carried by his Chamberlain. Of the other three figures immediately behind England's King, he whose face has been sliced away but on whose right shoulder the gauntleted hand of the tallest familiarly rests, is probably Shakespeare's 'false, fleeting, perjur'd Clarence'. In contrast to the uniform glumness of the French beyond the barrier, the English look positively jovial.

The left supporter (31) to this huge centrepiece (the seat measures 3ft 7in across) shows Louis XI (or Philippe de Commines impersonating him) emerging with his party onto a little bridge defended by a small cannon, from a castellated gateway. The right one (32) has Edward IV with orb and sceptre, smiling faces all around, leaving the Royal tent's doorway, which is surmounted by three banners of St George. The composition is surrounded at top and sides by unseasonable flowers—daffodils.

ANIMALS

INVERTEBRATES are rare on misericords. Entomologists must make do with Exeter's beetles (52), apparently stylised carabids. Other groups are represented not for their own sake but as, for example, heraldic symbols (132) or monster substitutes (50). Vertebrates of most major groups occur. Fish range from a percoid soul-symbol (100) to pike (53) and the sailfish-derived sea monster at Bishop's Stortford (54). Birds abound. The heron from Herne (an archaic spelling of heron) has for supporters what may be the earliest recognised leg-rings from any free-living bird (55). Such banding was undertaken before the release of captured but unharmed herons. The earliest recorded recovery date is 1710, but the ring, assumed to be silver, was not described.[36]

The Etchingham crane (58), previously misidentified as a hawk, shows typically long inner secondary wing feathers, bunchy back feathers, a long tail, strong hind claw and one-legged stance. Likewise Worcester's wood-cock (60) has until now been called a dove. However, although seemingly pointed when viewed directly from above, its broad and rather stumpy wings are actually rounded at the tip, as is proper for woodcock, when seen from the carver's angle. The bluntly rounded tail hardly extending beyond the wings and the overall projectile-like appearance support this identification; and as the long woodcock bill is angled downwards in flight, the apparently short one here, portrayed from above, presents no problem.

Up to now the true identity of the Exeter (63) and Wells (62) paired birds—the latter among the masterpieces of misericord carving—has not been realised. Despite some superficial resemblance to parrots, the slight crossing of the formers' mandibles at the tips, the fact that the top mandible is not conspicuously over-riding the lower in any of them, and the lack of a notably long and divided tail, eliminates England's only early mediaeval pet parrot, India's ring-necked parakeet, *Psittacula krameri*.[59] Our subject is evidently the conifer-breeding cone-opening crossbill, large numbers of which sporadically irrupt into England from Scandinavia, the first recorded appearance having been in 1251;[38] a 'nine days' wonder' that might well have accounted for the choice of the subject at Exeter very shortly afterwards.

No. 65 obviously illustrates some forgotten story or proverb. On the other supporter the sparrows, now wearing loaded packs, are approaching a post-windmill—perhaps having been forced to work for the miller in return for stealing grain.

Proportion is something never to be relied on in misericords. Neverthe-less, if the victim in No. 67 is actually a hare, only a gyr falcon could have taken it. In Nos. 69 and 70 it looks as if a talented carver deliberately selected the smallest European duck to suit his elegant design. An undoubted (because unmistakably coloured) gyr falcon that has struck down a mallard drake is seen in No. 68 from a mediaeval artist's pattern book,[34] and comparison of the two compositions strongly suggests that the same species of predator was involved. If you lie on the floor to

30

determine the angle from which the carver worked, his masterpiece really comes alive. It is one of the finest naturalistic achievements in English misericords of the later Decorated Period.

Among all these carvings, there are more examples of 'the Pelican in her Piety' (71) than any other identifiable bird. The legend, probably deriving from Ancient Egypt, has the parent bird being provoked to kill its young. Afterwards, in an agony of remorse, she bites her breast until blood flows to restore the nestlings to life—thus symbolising Man's Redemption through Christ's blood.

There has been much argument over whether hedgehogs behave in the manner depicted on No. 83. A BBC TV documentary recently seen by 12 million[44] aired the matter, without significant audience response. The facts are that these engaging animals neither take food back to their young in the nest, nor hoard it in winter.[44]

The rhinocerised hippopotamus of No. 80 may well be an attempt to portray Job's biblical Behemoth of the Jordan. Being lanceolate, sinuous and slightly serrate, the three leaves above the beast's head suggest that indeed 'the willows of the brook compass him about' (*Job* 40:22). This makes the supporter one of the tiny proportion linked to the centrepiece: in this case, SS Zosimus and Mary of Egypt.[33] The plants above the elephant in No. 81 may well be mandrakes. For the bestiaries assert that for their rare copulations, a pair of mandrake-eating elephants will journey as far eastwards as possible, 'than they come by eche other and engendreth be the way of nature . . .'[31]

The History of Reynard the Fox was the mediaeval equivalent of today's serial soap opera. The crafty hero-villain variously embarrassed and outwitted stronger animals like the wolf, bear and lion. He could suffer apparent death then enjoy resurrection. And there was always the sequel, including *The Shifts of Reynardine*, his son's adventures. This epic was born about 1150, with versions proliferating throughout Europe.[56] Reynard's doings were illustrated in manuscripts, stained glass and (doubtless) lost murals, as well as woodcarvings. However, only a minority of the episodes are actually represented. Some were especially popular, such as the portrayal of Reynard's departure with the goose (92, 93) on one of the farmyard forays that led to the Beast-epic. This is best represented at Bristol (94–97) in a fine series postdating by four decades the first English printed version, published by William Caxton in 1481 in a translation from the Dutch.

PLANTS AND HERALDRY

P LANTS comprise almost half of the entire British misericord subject matter. However, most of the plants that were carved are either quite unspecific decorative elements in centrepieces, or supporters so conventionalised as to defy unravelling into their plant components. Hence the very limited nature of this section. Even in the early phase of the Decorated Period, the late 13th-century subject (122) in Westminster Abbey is still only classifiable as 'conventionalised foliage'. Whether it is intended for water avens (*Geum rivale*, once called holy herb),[13] clover (*Trifolium* sp.) or Viollet-le-Duc's 'unopened leaves and buds of early spring'[12] is immaterial. This direct copy from Roman stonework stands for the Holy Trinity. Its leaves are now beginning to display the slightly bulged lobes of Geometrical/Decorated Art.[13] Trefoil increasingly shared the composition with cinquefoil (*Potentilla* sp.) in the more conservative carvings such as the present one. Nevertheless, decidedly more naturalistic work was already being done at Exeter, in what (at least in so far as we know) was the early dawn of English misericord carving. Examples include the marguerite (*Chrysanthemum leucanthemum*) and rose (*Rosa* sp., possibly the wild double eglantine, *R. rubiginosa*) which are the left and right supporters respectively of No. 25. In this mid 13th-century carving the ray-florets (left) and petals (right) already show the bulge of the new style developing from the flat forms of Early English botanical decoration.

However, except for a few other precursors such as the common oak (*Quercus robur*) leaves and acorns of No. 52 (Exeter), most foliage subjects are unidentifiable until the naturalism of the Decorated Period gathers momentum. Then, as early as 1305 (123) the roundish, finely toothed leaves and nuts invested by irregularly toothed bracts of the hazel (*Corylus avellana*) are clearly recognizable at Winchester Cathedral. In the past, these have been mistaken for beech. By the late 14th century, naturalism—which had bulged and rippled the oak leaves of No. 124 from Lincoln to the point where they were a world away from the Exeter (52) ones of a century earlier, was shading into the conventionalism destined to render most English misericord plant subjects delightfully ornamental but botanically hard to identify.

Previously identified no more specifically than 'water-flowers',[48] No. 121 shows what was probably a sample (freshly collected from the nearest stream) of the abundant opposite-leaved pondweed, *Groenlandia densa*. The circlet surrounds floating leaves of the yellow water-lily, *Nuphar lutea*, amongst which the fruits are hard to determine. They could be those of *G. densa*. No. 127 resembles an early herbal illustration, with its form-alised conception of a plant, roots and all. This is not a herb, though. It has trunk, branches and branchlets. From the toothed leaflets it seems to be the ash, *Fraxinus excelsior*, the young leaves of which were held to repel snakes[29,53] while their juice, 'being dranck with wine & applyed as a Cataplasme does help sych as are bitten by vipers'.[27] The presence of an exotic North African horned viper (*Cerastes cornutus*) is so odd as to render it most likely that the source was an early printed herbal if not a still earlier painted manuscript.

Up to now the subject of No. 128 from Denston in Suffolk has been identi-fied as acanthus leaves but it is more likely to be the Scotch thistle. All the supporters in this church are Tudor roses and the thistle may be a reference to the marriage of Henry VII's daughter Margaret to James IV of Scotland in 1503.

The Arms of Thomas Arundel, Bishop of Ely and later Archbishop of Canterbury, are displayed (129) at All Souls, Landbeach, in Cam-bridgeshire. This together with three others came from Jesus College, Cam-bridge in the late 18th century.[48] All four are typical of the early 15th century. Their dates are unknown, but the Archbishop died in 1414. His Arms are supported by formalised cinquefoils: *bordure engrailed; quarterly, one and four checky* (Warenne), *two and three lion rampant* (Fitzalan).[48] Here are also found the Arms of an earlier Bishop (de Lisle) of Ely (1345–61): *bordure, a fess between two chevrons*. In this instance the supporters are not lizards,[48] but wyverns (131). The chevron is one of the most ancient of symbols. The Shield of Calverley, an ancient Yorkshire family, is on one of the sixty-two late 14th-century misericords of New College Chapel, Oxford: *a fess between three calves, two and one* (130).[48] Rarely, Arms appear as elements in broader compositions, those of Peckham (*three crosslets patée; on a chief, a crescent*) in No. 35 for example.

1 A lady hawking, with peregrine falcon and spaniel. May or October in the Occupations of the Months sequence (Lincoln). (p. 25).

2 Childish games—mock battle and the hobby horse. Also January in the Ages of Man sequence (Sherborne). (p. 23).

3 Reaping corn, August in the Occupations of the Months sequence. Originally each figure seems to have had a sickle in one hand and a wooden crook, to hold the corn correctly, in the other (Ripple). (p. 24).

4 Carting corn sheaves, August. Associated mummery illustrated in the supporters (Victoria & Albert Museum). (p. 24).

5 The earliest-known reaping machine, the month of August and the proverb warning against putting the cart before the horse may well all be subjects of this 1520 Beverley Minster misericord. Note the ripe heads of grain into which the cutter/tearer end of the open farmwagon is being pushed, also (right supporter) England's only misericord milking scene (p. 25).

6 Disembowelling the slaughtered pig, November (sometimes December). The alleged rabbits (or mice?) that are this carver's trademark leave and enter burrows under the table (Bristol). (p. 25).

7 The Good Shepherd (Winchester College). (p. 25).

8 Childish games, handball. January in the Ages of Man sequence (Gloucester).
   (p. 23).

10 Indoor domestic scene, winter (February or December): he with his mittens, she with her distaff and cat (Ripple). (p. 24).

9 The tapster (Ludlow). (p. 25).

11 As two gamblers quarrel, the tavern cat takes refuge on the coffer to the right (Windsor). (p. 26).

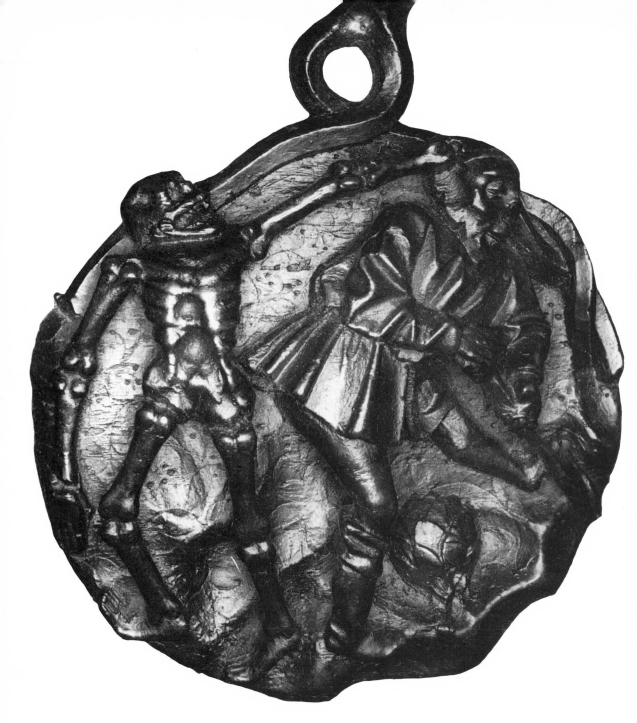

12 Death comes for the labourer: Dance of Death sequence (Windsor). (p. 26).

13 Domestic brawl, wife close to victory (Carlisle).

14 Merrymaking—the contortionist or posture-maker with his hands on his knees (Hereford, All Saints).

15 (Left) Paying for favours. Adapted from the
   print below (16) by Dürer, ca 1495
   (Westminster). (p. 21).

17 The rape. Adapted from the print below (18) by
   Dürer, ca 1495 (Westminster).

21 The joust, with the drummer in danger. Note 'snare' of catgut, the vibrating
   cord stretched across the parchment of his 'nakers' or kettledrums
   (Worcester). (p. 27).

19 Merrymaking—the snatched kiss (Chichester). (p. 26).

20 Role reversal. Miserably clutching a winding frame and ball of wool, a man
   is birched on his bare buttocks by a woman. This may be a reference to
   Hercules' enslavement to Omphale, Queen of Lydia (Westminster). (p. 26).

22 The siege. The left supporter is cocking his crossbow, holding the bolt under his chin and sheltering behind a shield. The other besieger is holding a *baston à feu* or hand-cannon. These had already been used for a hundred years before this was carved, but as his attitude shows, there was always the prospect of them blowing up in your face (Windsor).

23 An incident from the legend of Sir Yvain. Galloping into the castle in pursuit of his enemy, he has been trapped inside as the dropped portcullis impales his horse. The detached supporters show the two men-at-arms who come into the story (Chester). (p. 27).

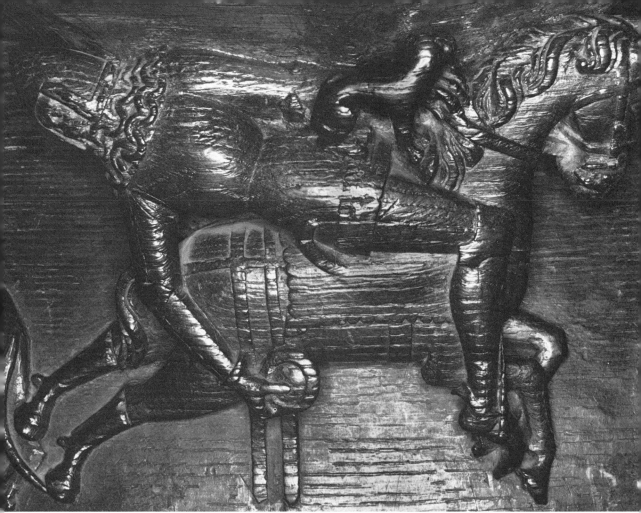

24 Using the technique advocated by Pliny and the mediaeval bestiaries, this knight drops a mirror intended to delay the pursuing tigress (27, below opposite) whose cub he is stealing (Chester). (p. 28).

25 The Swan Knight. The legendary hero of the First Crusade whose fame was perpetuated in England by the badge of the de Bohuns and who became the inspiration for Wagner's *Lohengrin* (Exeter). (pp. 19, 27).

26 Tristan and Iseult, whose husband King Mark watches the lovers through
the branches of the sheltering tree, at whose foot Iseult's dog is the first to
see him reflected in the pool (Chester). (p. 28).

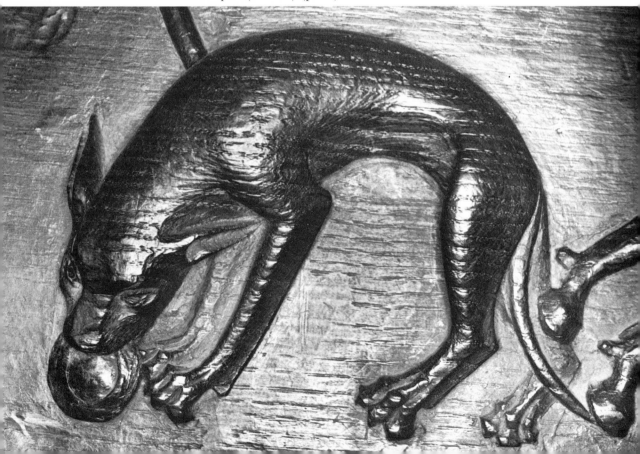

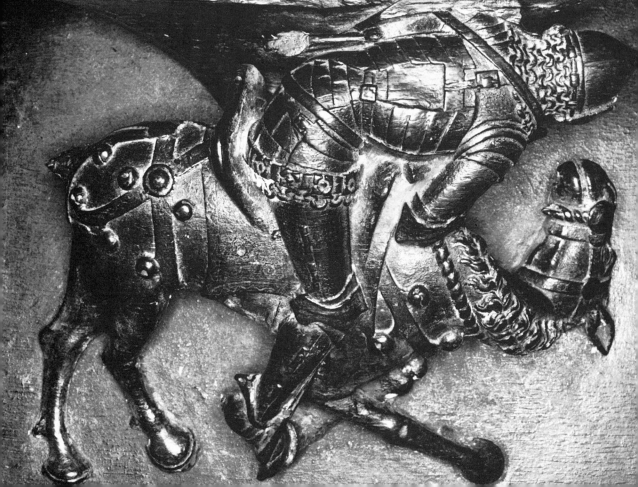

30 King Edward IV meets (the now headless) Louis XI of France on the bridge specially built over the Somme for the occasion at Picquigny, near Amiens, 29 August 1475—the only dateable contemporary event on any misericord. 31 Left, supporter to 30, the royal party of France emerge from a castellated gateway to meet the English. 32, Right supporter to 30, King Edward IV comes from the royal tent, surmounted by its three banners of St George and with daffodils all around (Windsor). (p. 28).

28 (above, opposite) Dismounted knight spearing wild boar and drawing his dagger to finish it off (Beverley, St Mary).

29 (below, opposite) With a crossbow bolt in his back, this knight sags in the saddle as his charger collapses (Lincoln). (p. 28).

33 Who is the lady vigorously dispatching this lion? The female head of the left supporter wears the wimple in vogue in the 14th century and earlier, which later became restricted to nuns (Chichester).

34 Naked lady, rose-branch in hand, mounted on a stag in the woods. Representing the 'orrible synne of luxurie' (Stratford-upon-Avon).

35 Death of the unicorn—the usual method seen here required a virgin as live bait (Stratford-upon-Avon). 36 Another way of dealing with unicorns—having used himself as bait the hunter ducks behind a tree, and his pursuer's horn becomes fixed in the trunk (Cartmel).

37 In the ancient tale of the Clever Daughter, she is soon to gain the king's
hand by having solved his riddle and come to him neither driving nor
walking nor riding (she's only half-seated on the goat), neither dressed nor
naked (thus draped in a fishnet), neither out of the road nor in the road
(only her right big toe touches the ground) and bearing a gift that's no gift
(the hare will leap off on release). (Worcester)[39].

38 It seems likely that the dual themes of the Locusts of the Apocalypse (*Rev. IX*, 7–10) and Aristotle saddled up to be ridden by Campaspe for whose charms he fell after cautioning a pupil, the young Alexander, against her, were meant to be conveyed by this misericord's designer (Exeter).

39 Urging on a slow horse—nicknamed 'sky slug' in the old Somerset dialect. The glass-snail (*Vitrina* sp.) represents a burdened packhorse (Bristol).

40 The lance-notch at the top-right of this man's shield suggests that he is meant for a dismounted knight despite his rather ambivalent costume. He seems to be attempting to rescue a lamb from a mythical griffin (Norwich).

41 A Barbary ape holding up the urine flask of mediaeval medical diagnosis, between a cleric offering a long-cross silver penny on the left and a secular figure with an object resembling the modern American doughnut on the right (Beverley, St Mary).

42 The legendary Flight of Alexander, seen here seated between the griffins that bore him aloft to see for himself where sea and sky meet at the ends of the earth. Appropriately, the supporters here show Traveller's Joy! (Wells).

43 Merrymaking—jesters with cats as
   bagpipes (Boston).

44 Merrymaking—man with pig as bagpipes
   (Lavenham).

45, 46 Two rather mysterious scenes from
   Bristol, one of bear baiting and the other,
   possibly a satire on chivalry, of a man
   fighting armed rat-like beasts and hitting
   one on his back-swing. Why are the men
   naked?

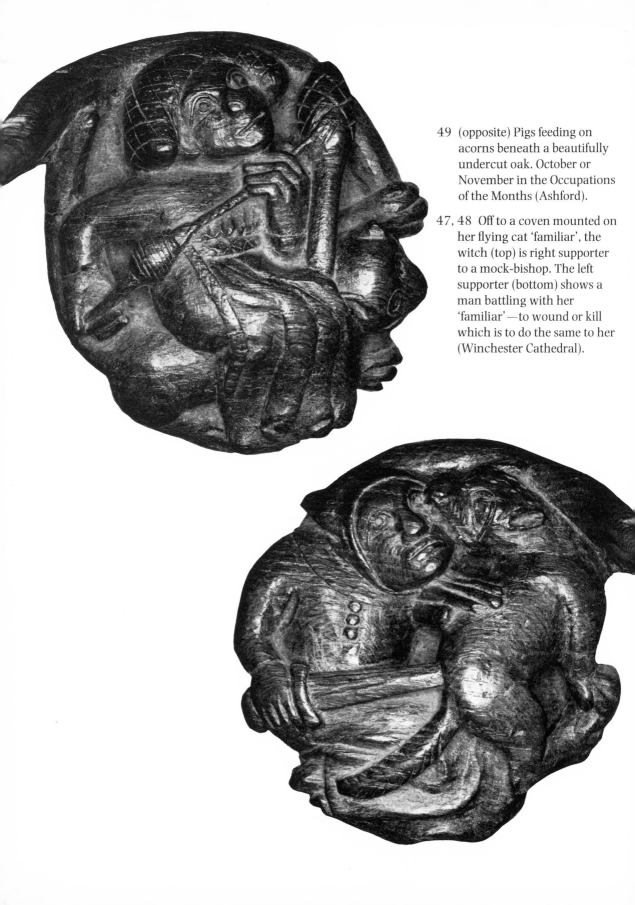

49 (opposite) Pigs feeding on acorns beneath a beautifully undercut oak. October or November in the Occupations of the Months (Ashford).

47, 48 Off to a coven mounted on her flying cat 'familiar', the witch (top) is right supporter to a mock-bishop. The left supporter (bottom) shows a man battling with her 'familiar'—to wound or kill which is to do the same to her (Winchester Cathedral).

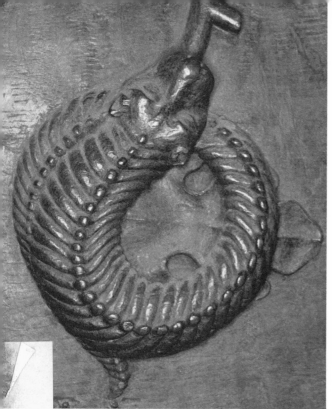

51 Zoologically lamentable frog, three toes and with all feet equally webbed (Edlesborough). (p. 19).

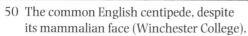

50 The common English centipede, despite its mammalian face (Winchester College).

52 The only 'green man' illustrated is not altogether typical of his kind, the face being a satyr's mask and acorns and oak leaves sprouting from the crown. The supporters feature more of the latter but with beetles curled within them. These oak beetles are the only identifiable insects on any English misericord (Exeter). (pp. 19, 29).

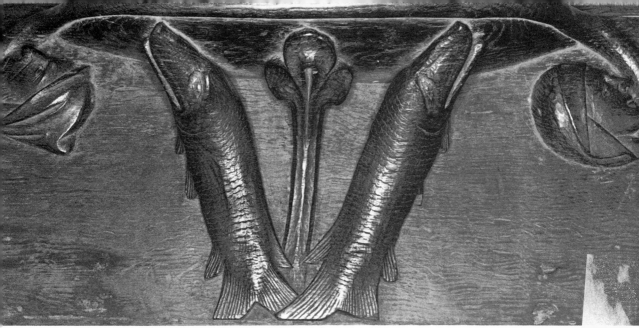

53 Two pike of possibly heraldic significance, although naturalistically represented. Hooded heads of man and woman as supporters (Exeter).

54 Sailfish-Serra, the conventional leaf supporters in this instance perhaps modelled to resemble skates? (Bishop's Stortford).

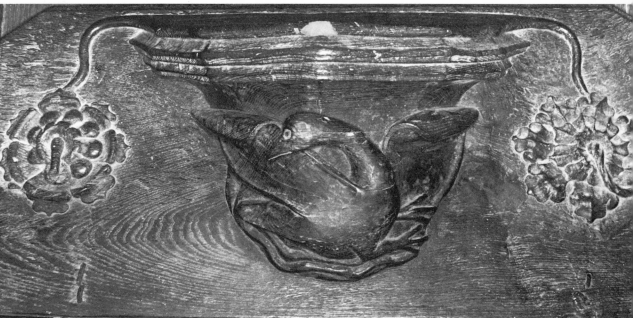

55 Heron, nuptial plumes displayed, alighting on water; ornamented leg-bands as supporters. 56 Late 19th-century attempted copy, misinterpreting the bird as a duck and the leg-bands as flowers (Herne). (p. 30).

57 Sentinel crane, clutching the stone that will drop and awaken it should it doze off on guard duty (Denston).

58 Crane feeding (Etchingham). (p. 30).

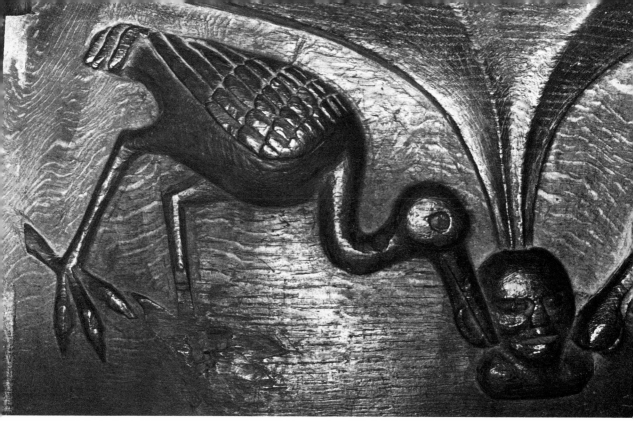

59 Ibis in its bestiary role of corpse-eater. The beak of a spoonbill is on the right (Lavenham).

60 A woodcock, supporter to a sower, the prime symbol of March, the month when northward-bound woodcock were netted (Worcester). (p. 30).

61 This eel-grasping ibis is identified by its decurved bill (Windsor).

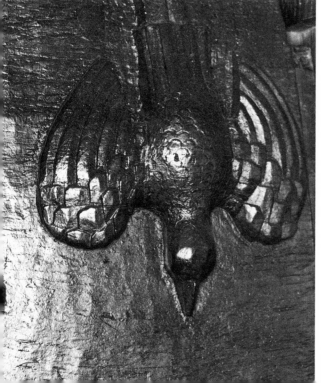

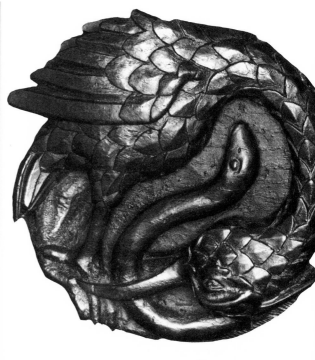

62, 63 Common crossbills, those below having been previously identified as doves or parrots (Exeter), and those above as parrots (Wells, p. 30). The ones at Exeter were carved within two decades of the first recorded irruption of common crossbills into southern England; those at Wells are shown in the species' favourite tree, the Scots Pine.

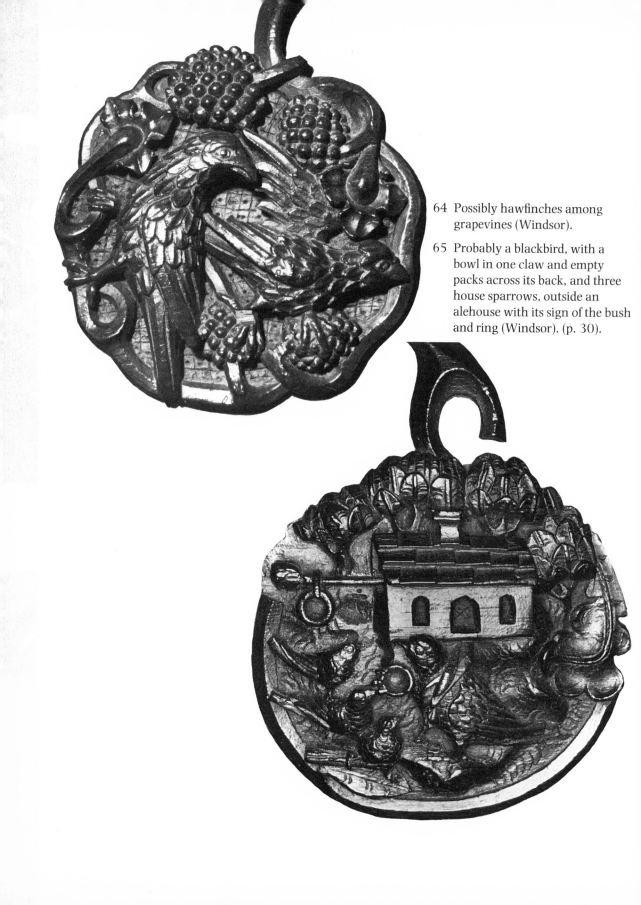

64 Possibly hawfinches among grapevines (Windsor).

65 Probably a blackbird, with a bowl in one claw and empty packs across its back, and three house sparrows, outside an alehouse with its sign of the bush and ring (Windsor). (p. 30).

66 The mobbing of an owl in a grapevine by small passerine birds symbolized a sinner under attack by the righteous, or outright anti-semitism; the owl being the Jew who preferred darkness to Christian light, and his persecutors the Gentiles (Norwich).

67 A gyr falcon on the brown hare that it's been flown at? (Wells). (p. 30).

68 Gyr falcon on mallard, from the only surviving pattern-book from an artists' workshop of mediaeval England (late 14th-century, the Pepysian sketchbook, Magdalene College, Cambridge).

69 Probably a gyr falcon on a teal (Winchester College). (p. 30).

70 Detail of 69 from carver's angle, bringing out the quality of this small masterpiece.

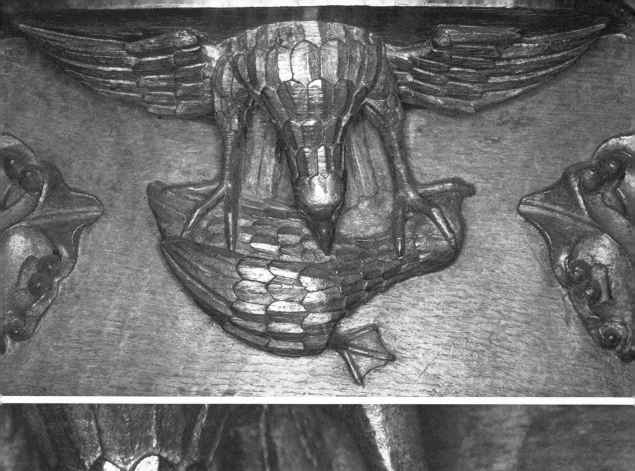

71 The Pelican in her Piety, a favourite mediaeval symbol of self-sacrifice, particularly of the Redemption. Always resembling the bestiary concept rather than the natural bird and its clumsy nest, the so-called pelican is shown feeding her young with her blood after ripping her breast (Gloucester). (p. 31).

72 An ostrich as described by the *Physiologus*, with cloven feet (explaining its speed in running) and a voracious appetite extending to horseshoes (Stratford-upon-Avon).

73 Greater horseshoe bat, doubling for the Devil and very possibly at least partly modelled on the woodcut in 74 as well as on a freshly dead specimen (Christchurch). (p. 20).

74 Head of Devil/greater horseshoe bat represented as glaring from an early 14th-century Armenian rock overhang from Sir John Mandeville's *Travels*.[41] Resemblances of expression, ears and hair fringe details suggest that the carver of 73 was influenced by the woodcut first published three decades earlier.

75 Possibly meant for a piebald example of Britain's most abundant bat, the common pipistrelle (Cambridge, St John's College).

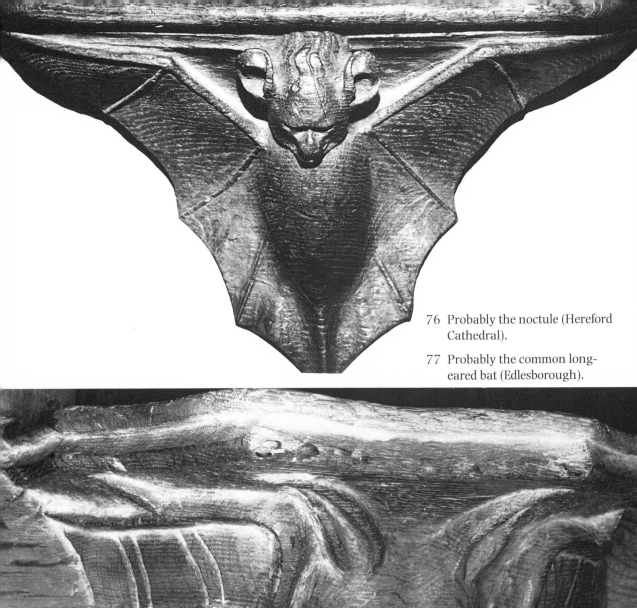

76 Probably the noctule (Hereford Cathedral).

77 Probably the common long-eared bat (Edlesborough).

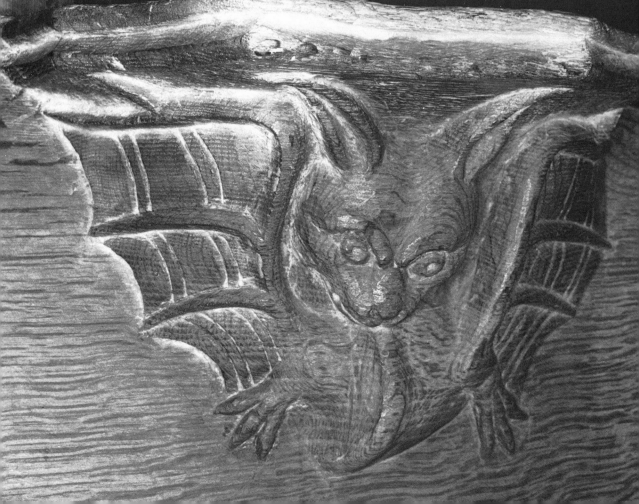

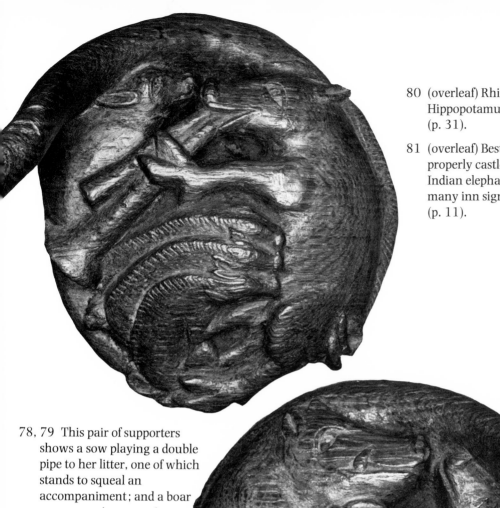

80 (overleaf) Rhinocerised Hippopotamus (Windsor). (p. 31).

81 (overleaf) Bestiary version of a properly castled (howdah'd) Indian elephant, ancestor of many inn signs (Windsor). (p. 11).

78, 79 This pair of supporters shows a sow playing a double pipe to her litter, one of which stands to squeal an accompaniment; and a boar accompanying a porcine vocalist on the viol (Winchester Cathedral). (p. 18).

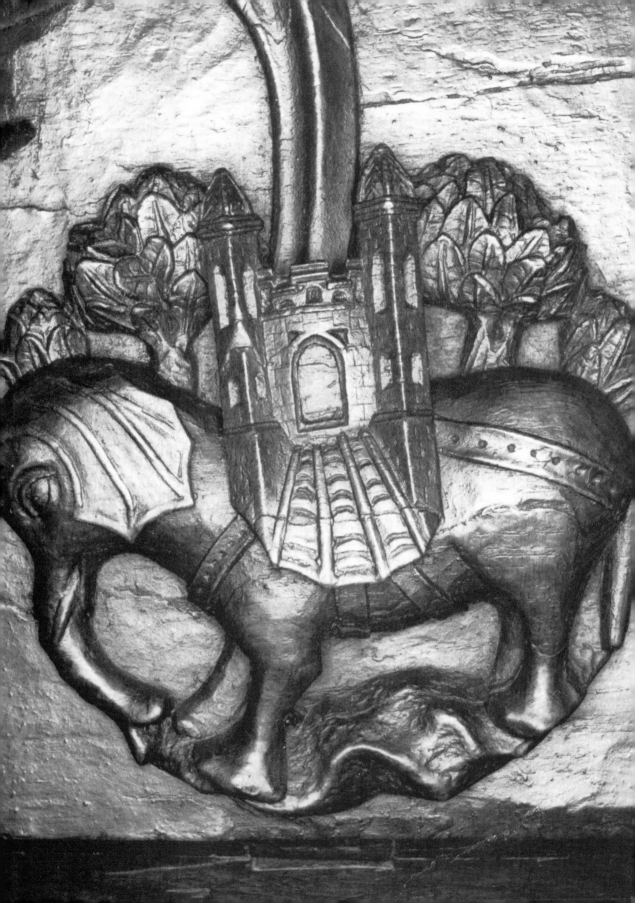

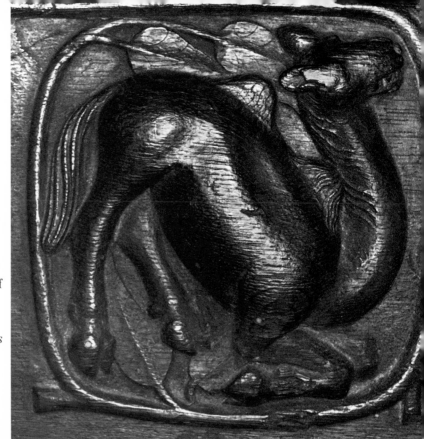

82 Female Bactrian camels kneel for several reasons according to the *Physiologus* and the bestiaries. For Adoration, humility and as a plea for copulation. All three meanings would certainly have been read into this best of all camel carvings on English misericords, by the rather small handful of mediaeval people who actually saw it (Boston).

83 Illustrating the *Physiologus* tale about hedgehogs impaling grapes or apples on their spines, to carry them back to the nest (Oxford, New College). (p. 31).

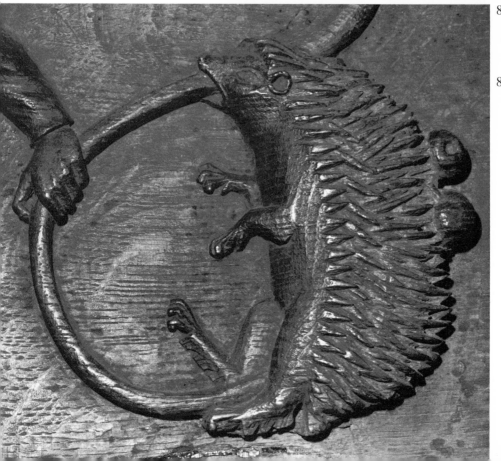

84 One of the commoner mammalian subjects, a lion's head (Oxford, All Souls).

85 Bestiary hyena feeding on a disinterred corpse; vice feeding on corruption (Carlisle).

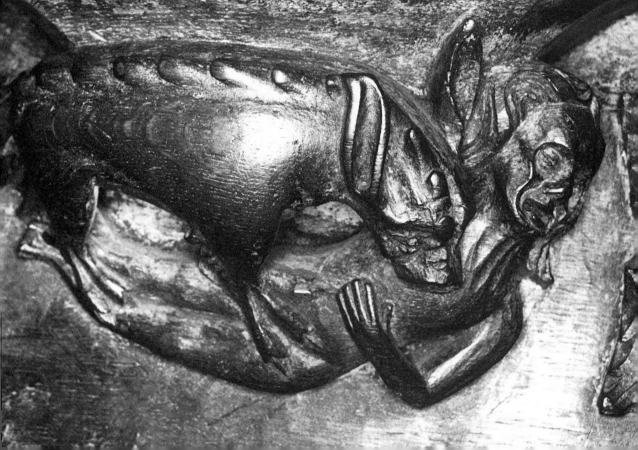

86 Bestiary wolfs punish
a foot by biting it, for
having made a noise
and alerted the prey –
and licked it, to silenc
its tread (Faversham)

87 Another wolf acting c
its bestiary role has
attacked a man who
failed to see it first; so
he's been struck dum
and is screaming
soundlessly for help
(Winchester Cathedr;

88 Rabbit at bay, perhap
because four other
misericords in this
church show predato
(Old Malton).

89 Hare mounted on hound, an example of the topsy-turvy theme so dear to mediaeval hearts (Worcester). (p. 18).

90 Otter with captured fish (Windsor).

91 Renhound, today's greyhound, clearly in need of a better bone than the dry one it's gnawing (Christchurch).

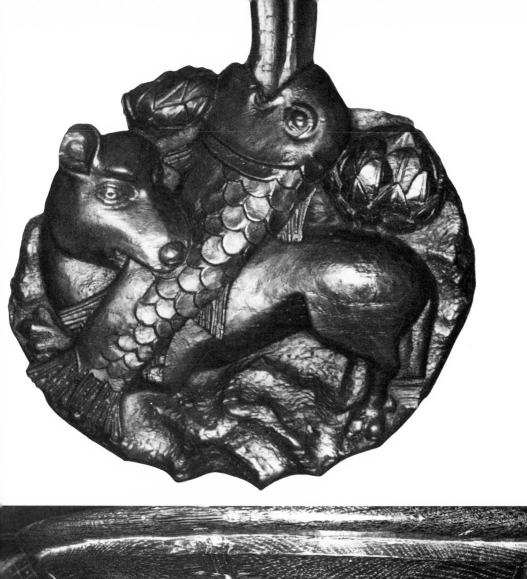

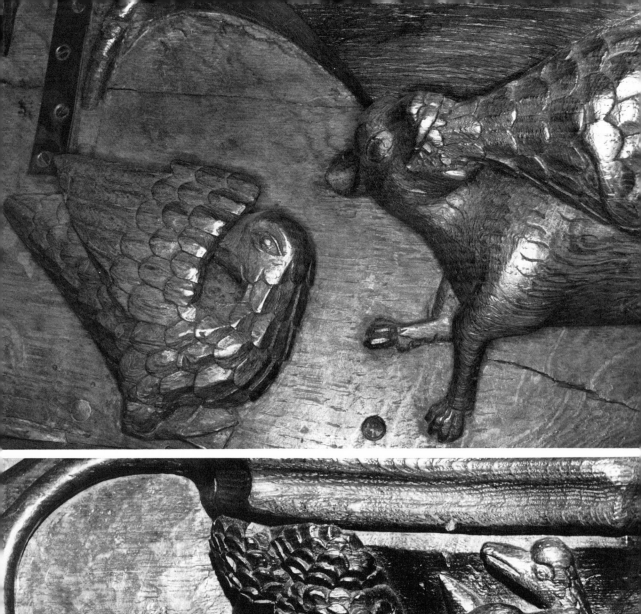

92 Robbing a farmyard as in 93, this natural fox has only another goose to pass; and it, on the left supporter, is intent upon seeing no evil and staying out of trouble (Winchester College). (p. 31).

93 Reynard must now escape the shouldered distaff of the farmer's wife, crouching in ambush, before gaining the woods suggested by the stylised trees of the centrepiece background (Ripon).

94 Fresh from bed Mertynet the priest has a testicle ripped away by the Cat Tybert, manoeuvered into a snare by Reynard who's now watching in amusement. The priest's equally naked son holds the rope of the snare; his wife, who can't keep the grin off her face, is swinging her distaff at Tybert (Bristol). (p. 20).

95 For a mounting series of crimes Reynard was tried and sentenced to death. Here are King Noble the Lion with his Queen Fière watching the Fox being led off to execution (Bristol).

96 Gleeful at the outcome, Isegrim and Bruin the Bear (who had suffered great injury thanks to Reynard) dance hand-in-hand around a bush, to the beat of an ape drummer. (Bristol).

97 Had the hanging actually taken place the job would have been reserved for the Geese (there are several versions of the tale; sometimes Reynard dies, or appears to, and is resurrected—the symbolism is obvious) (Bristol).

98 The Fox, attired as a friar, preaches on many misericords to a congregation of poultry—usually geese. One of the six seen here is obviously a born loser (Etchingham). (p. 9).

99 (Previous page) Hell-mouth (Ludlow).

100 The acquiescent fish clasped by this earliest (1250–60) of English misericord mermaids symbolises the soul in the grip of earthly passion, as did the vanished one in her other hand (Exeter).

101 Mermaids suckling lions are probably conveying a message about inherent evil and invincible strength. There are three other similar misericords in England (Hereford Cathedral).

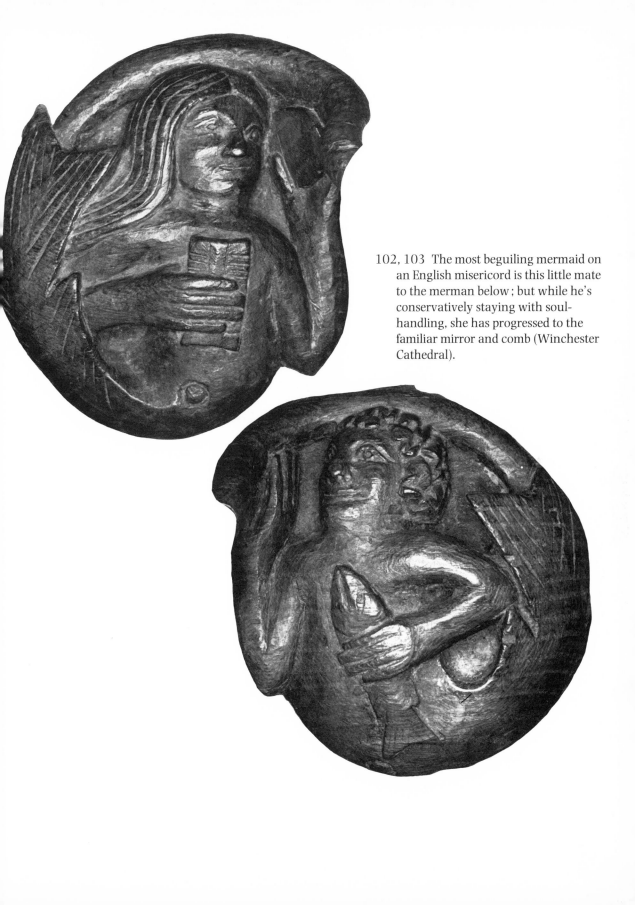

102, 103 The most beguiling mermaid on an English misericord is this little mate to the merman below; but while he's conservatively staying with soul-handling, she has progressed to the familiar mirror and comb (Winchester Cathedral).

104 This mermaid too has abandoned the pre-Christian role of a conveyor of souls to Hades for the more aggressive one of the seductress keeping up her image with mirror and comb (Lincoln).

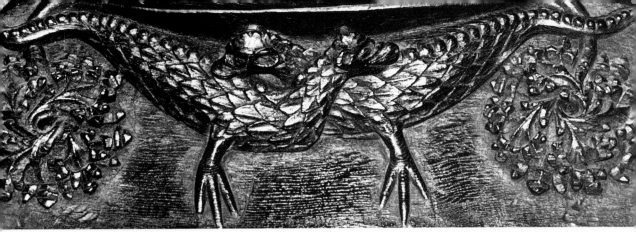

105 The evolution of the winged, four-legged dragon starts with a wingless, two-legged reptilian creature, the lindworm (Hereford, All Saints).

106 Although still two-legged, the wyvern is winged. Most English "dragons" are properly wyverns like the pair seen here below another representation of the Flight of Alexander, not to be confused with the supporting griffins on either side of the king—see No. 42 (Beverley, St Mary).

107 A double-headed wyvern shepherding three damned souls to their fate (Bristol).

108 Woodcut from *The Grete Herball* of the 1520s, which had already appeared in other printed books. Reversed, this was the source of the design for 107, although the carver failed to achieve the pose of the figure nearest the wyvern and instead twisted its head beyond the point of anatomical feasibility.[14] It was also the source for a stone bas-relief in the de La Warr Chantry at Boxgrove in Sussex.

109 Mask of a faun or Pan himself, doubling as the Devil: a powerful renaissance carving (Cambridge, King's College).

110 Demon eavesdropping as two
women gossip in church. One of
six similar English misericords.
The left supporter (not illus.)
shows the demon Tutivillus
writing down what was said.
(London, Stepney). (p. 20)

111 A siren wearing a mediaeval
woman's horned head-dress, the
hennin (at the height of fashion
towards the mid 15th century—
this was carved in 1445). Her
supporters are basilisks (Ludlow).

112 Another siren, this one with bird
wings, and the addition of a North
African horned viper perhaps
intended for an amphisbaena tail
(Winchester College).

113 Crowned swan-like monster with
a woman's face and bat wings.
Possibly alluding to the Swan
Knight legend (No. 25) and/or the
pet whooper swan of St Hugh
(Lincoln).

114 Birdperson couple perhaps symbolising newly married bliss (Exeter).

115 Basilisk, half cock and half serpent, being confronted by a weasel, immune from the monster's otherwise fatal glance and bite because it carries a sprig of rue in its mouth (Worcester).

116 Puckish mask, but with bossed horns of a bull (Stratford-upon-Avon).

117 The giant of the Jack-and-the-beanstalk folktale, grasping farm livestock. Jack hides in one supporter and his mother is on the other. (Oxford, New College).

120 Blemya tiptoeing up to a man who appears to have just discovered hockey, but who is actually one of a centrepiece pair threshing wheat—either July or August in the Occupations of the Months. The standard Blemya had its facial features on its torso but this one is a legged head (Victoria & Albert Museum).

118 Hieronymus Bosch had only been dead some twenty years when this unique monster was carved (1533–38), conjuring up the Temptation of St Anthony and Apocalyptic dreadfulness (Cambridge, King's College). (p. 22)

119 A Wodehouse, the mythical wild man of the forest, in need of a lion's skin (Hereford Cathedral).

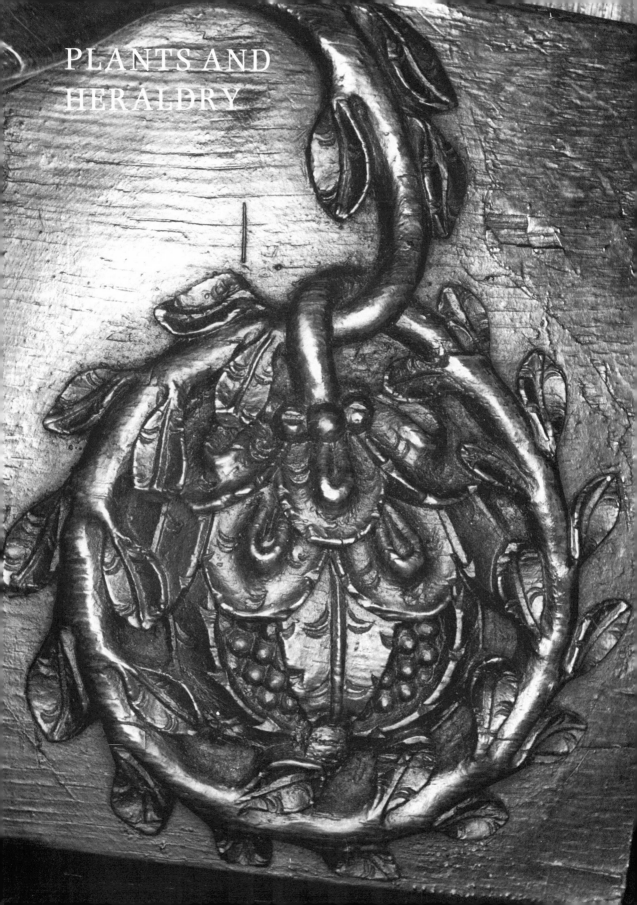

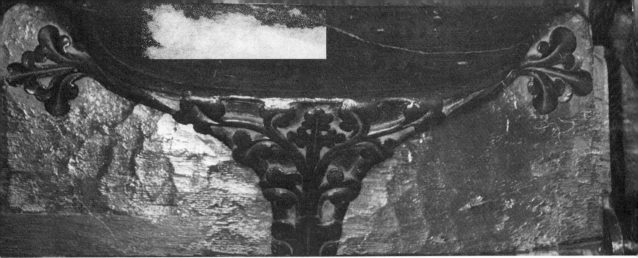

122 The only misericord of the original 13th-century set preserved when
Henry VII's Chapel was established in Westminster Abbey, was this
conventionalised foliage of the Geometric/Decorated Period—slightly
bulged lobes of trefoil and cinquefoil. (p. 32)

121 Loop of opposite-leafed pondweed surrounding yellow water-lily leaves
(Windsor). (p. 33)

123 A hazel nut is being eaten by a red squirrel, among beautifully naturalistic
leaves and nuts, the realism of which characterises the early Curvilinear/
Decorated Period (Winchester Cathedral). (p. 32)

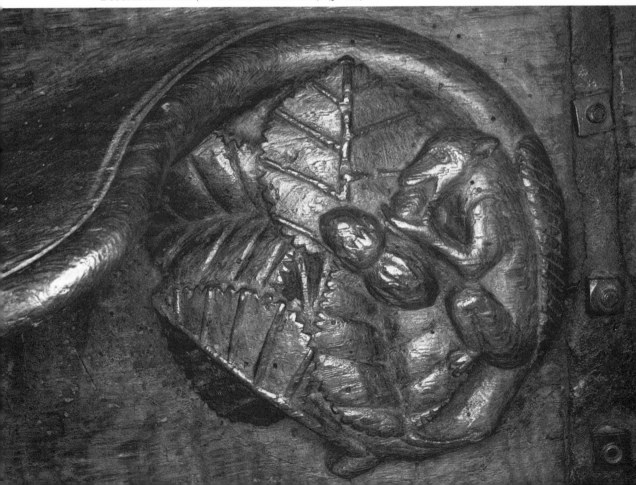

124 Developing conventionalism marks these oak leaf supporters to an eagle.
The latter was presumably carved from a manuscript illustration in which
the ball it is shown as clutching was properly represented as one of its own
downy nestlings—the bestiaries had eagles sharpening the eyesight of
their young by carrying them towards the sun (Lincoln).

125 The grapes being gathered for the vintage. Symbolises October in the
Occupations of the Months (Gloucester). (p. 25)

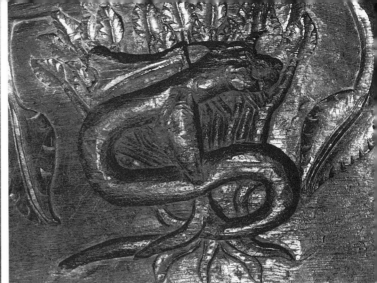

126 Rose badge of England, right supporter of two to fine bearded head of a
late 14th-century member of the House of Lancaster; later the emblem of
the Lancastrians in the Wars of the Roses (London, Stepney).

127 Ash tree, roots and all, the fresher shoots of leaves being thought
efficacious against snakes (the North African horned viper is shown) both
as an antidote and a repellent (Bampton-in-the-Bush). (p. 33)

128 Scotch thistle (Denston). (p. 33)

129 Arms of Thomas Arundel, 14th-century Bishop of Ely, Archbishop of York, twice Chancellor of England and Archbishop of Canterbury. The supporters represent conventionalised flowers of cinquefoil, then regarded as a cure for malaria—the ague of the fenlands of Cambridgeshire and elsewhere (Landbeach). (p. 33)

130 Shield of Calverley displaying naturalistic calves, left supporter to shield of Beauchamp of Warwick (Oxford, New College).

131 Arms of Bishop de Lisle of Ely, predecessor of Thomas Arundel. The supporters are wyverns (Landbeach).

132 Badge of Richard de Beauchamp, Bishop of Salisbury and Chancellor of the Order of the Garter, late 15th century; naturalistic snails on a mitre (Windsor).

133 Warwick badge of the Bear and Ragged Staff (Stratford-upon-Avon).

134 St Giles, the hermit Saint of Nîmes, comforting the hind he had befriended,
now wounded by an arrow in a royal hunt. The supporters show the
offending bowmen. One version of the legend indicates that the arrow
struck St Giles himself, in the knee. But in this carving the arrow has
clearly transfixed the hind's neck as far as its shaft feathers. The Saint's
position is such that he could only be straddling the arrow, which could
not possibly have pierced either of his knees. His right hand is caressing
his friend's flank, beneath the feathered wings of the arrow, the thumb
under the entry point (just beneath the hind's left ear and by his own
shins). (Ely).

THE BIBLE AND
THE SAINTS

135 The Expulsion from Paradise (Worcester).

136 Adam delving, Eve spinning (Victoria & Albert Museum).

137, 138, 139 Noah in his Ark, awaits the returning dove, with his supporters below: the raven gorging on drowned cattle and the dove with the olive branch (wrongly leaved). (Ely).

141 Samson bearing away the gates of Giza (Ripon). (p. 21)

140 Samson rending the lion's jaws (Norwich).

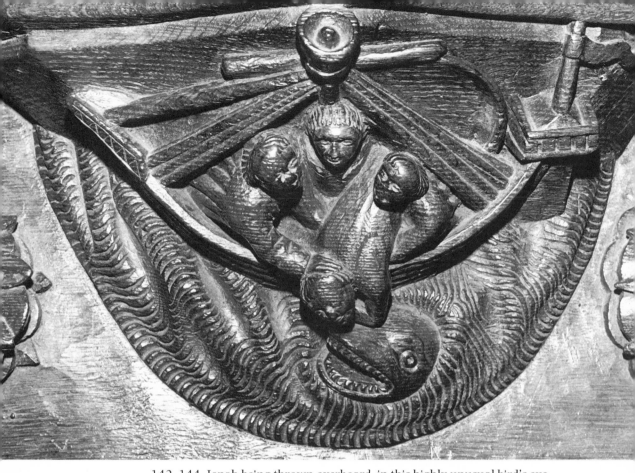

142, 144 Jonah being thrown overboard, in this highly unusual bird's eye
perspective which looks down into the ship's crow's nest, and then being
vomited ashore (right) to proceed to Nineveh, by the properly gilled 'great
fish' (Ripon).

143 Judith about to decapitate Holofernes. Foliate squares as supporters, and
note the diminutive roses, Lincoln's speciality, on the fore-edge of the
underseat ledge (Lincoln). (p. 27)

145 King Solomon is central to the design of h
Judgement, the dead child at his feet, a
mother on either side and a soldier ready
bisect the live baby.

146 Right supporter to 145, the mother of the
dead baby leaving it in place of the live on
she's stealing (London, Westminster).

147 St Margaret of Antioch giving thanks for
escape from the belly of the dragon that
materialised in a corner of her prison cell,
belching fire and speaking roughly, then
swallowed her. The cross-staff with which
vanquished the dragon/Satan is not evide
but she's clearly well enough to give than
for her deliverance as 'the proper saint to
invoked by women in the pangs of childbi
She had 261 English churches dedicated
her. (Sherborne).

148 (below) In the Arabian desert the naked St Mary of Egypt is seen still trying
     to secure the promised protection of St Zosimus' mantle. We are given to
     understand that in about 430 Zosimus took this reformed public prostitute
     for a holy anchorite. At first she ran away but eventually agreed to talk
     to him in return for his cloak. The left supporter to this scene is the
     hippopotamus, No. 81 (Windsor).

151 Not a Saint, but perhaps a welcomer of one to his or her reward: Angelic
     piper (London, Stepney).

149 Having not only stolen but also cooked one of the wild geese to which St
     Werburga offered protection, in return for their leaving the crops alone in
     future, this servant of hers is apprehended (Chester).

150 The entire misericord from which 149 is enlarged shows the miscreant's
     confession on the right supporter with the centrepiece illustrating the
     Saint's success in having the cooked goose resurrected.

HOW TO PHOTOGRAPH MISERICORDS

These carvings are difficult to photograph *in situ*. With rather few exceptions[23,35] past illustrations have done less than justice to them. The misericords are usually in dark places where the available lighting within the choir of the church cannot help very much in focussing, while the working position is usually cramped. Mediaeval clerics were somewhat smaller than we are and the space between rows of choir stalls is barely sufficient for sitting nowadays, so quite inadequate for the use of camera lenses of the usual focal lengths. I developed a system of using a light and easily manipulated torch for throwing a focussing spot onto the subject, and usually employed a 35 mm wide-angle lens so as to be able to take in the whole upturned seat when required. A macro lens was used in extremely close-up work and many of my pictures were taken with a ring-flash device (the compact and rapidly rechargeable Minicam mini-module) completely surrounding the lens and permitting unusually evenly lit negatives. Where contrast was required for dramatic effect, a hand-held electronic unit was used to achieve a grazed flash. My electronic flash gear permitted the use of a slow and virtually grainless monochrome film at a small enough aperture to obtain considerable depth of field, so that I could illustrate both the subject and the grain of the wood in the background. Sepia toning was found to give the best effect for comparative purposes, being close to the natural colour of old wood and yet providing a standard finish accommodating the often major differences between sets of misericords from different locations arising from age, varnishing technique used, etc. (giving an actual range from light brown to something little short of black).

In the past, because of the very constricted working conditions, too many photographs of misericords were taken face-on, from a squatting or kneeling position. This approach has its place, but for optimum results it must be generously supplemented by experimentation, lying on your back on the floor if necessary to find the angle that the carver worked from. Once you have done this, what at first sight seems a rather pedestrian effort can come alive with stunning force. Examples are Nos. 59, 60, and 'supping with the devil' here. In the case of the latter pair, from Windsor's St George's Chapel, the man supping with the Devil looks surly and foreshortened from the front, but alert and in good proportion when you find the angle from which the carver worked.

Just in case the reader has been put off by the thought of expensive camera equipment and ringflash gear, any modern SLR and electronic flash unit will serve for most purposes. A Canadian friend kindly photographed a misericord

from Dunblane Cathedral in Perthshire that I have never seen. The 35 mm colour transparency that she duly sent me was her first effort at misericord photography. The picture made from it, shows that despite its accurate wing support system (correct as to fingers, all proceeding from the wrist as they should), this bat falls somewhere half-way between a common pipistrelle and the serotine (*Eptesicus serotinus*), the tail of which is quite long and free as shown; while serotines are not found north of the Border nowadays, who knows whether they were in the mid 15th century?

LOCATIONS AND DATES OF MISERICORDS ILLUSTRATED

G. L. Remnant's *A Catalogue of Misericords in Great Britain* is acknowledged with appreciation as the source of this information, likewise of data on which the abbreviations after each plate number are based. These abbreviations (not given for some of the smaller collections) will facilitate finding the misericords illustrated. N, S, E and W obviously stand for the points of the compass (those unfamiliar with Christian churches should remember that the altar is always to the east of the choir, or chancel). U and L signify upper or lower as the case may be, where there are two rows of stalls with misericords on either side of the choir. The number following is that of the stall. E or W after it indicates whether the count should start from the east or west end. A terminal /EB or /WB signifies east or west block where the stalls are so subdivided. Abbreviations beginning RS refer to returned stalls. When these are present they are at right-angles to those aligned lengthwise, and face up the choir towards the altar from the west end. An N or S after a returned stall's number, indicates which side of the central aisle it is on.

ASHFORD (Kent). St Mary the Virgin, ca 1475: 49(N8E)

BAMPTON-IN-THE-BUSH (Oxon.). St Mary, early 16th C: 127(N1)

BEVERLEY (Humberside). Minster, 1520: 5(NU11W); St Mary, ca 1445: 28(N6W) 41(N3W) 106(N7W)

BISHOP'S STORTFORD (Herts). St Michael, probably 15th C: 54(S7E)

BOSTON (Lincs). St Botolphs, ca 1390: 43(NL8E) 82(SU17E)

BRISTOL (Avon). The Cathedral, 1515–26: 6(N6W) 39(S5W) 45(S9W) 46(S6W) 94(S3W) 95(N3W) 96(S10W) 97(N9W) 107(S7W)

CAMBRIDGE (Cambs). King's College Chapel, 1533–38: 109(S12W) 118(RSS3W); St John's College Chapel, early 16th C: 75(S20W)

CARLISLE (Cumbria). The Cathedral, 1399–1413: 13(S8W) 85(S18W)

CARTMEL (Cumbria). The Priory, ca 1440: 36(N13E)

CHESTER (Cheshire). The Cathedral, 1390: 23(S46) 24(N21W) 26(N19W) 149(N6W) 150(N6W)

CHICHESTER (W. Sussex). The Cathedral, ca 1330: 19(N7E) 33(S26)

CHRISTCHURCH (Hants). The Priory, 1515: 73 (NL5E) 91(NL11E)

DENSTON (Suffolk). St Nicholas, late 15th C: 57(N1) 128

EDLESBOROUGH (Bucks). St Mary the Virgin, 15th C: 51(N–S2) 77(N–S6)

ELY (Cambs). The Cathedral, ca 1340: 134 (SL18W) 137, 138, 139(SU3W)

ETCHINGHAM (E. Sussex). Assumption & St Nicholas, late 14th C: 58(N4) 98(S9)

EXETER (Devon). The Cathedral, mid 13th C: 25(S18) 38(N30) 52(S3) [1260–70] 53(N36) 63(N41) 100(N25) [1250–1260] 114(S6) [1240–1250]

FAVERSHAM (Kent). St Mary of Charity, late 15th C: 86(S7E)

GLOUCESTER (Glos). The Cathedral, mid 14th C: 8(SW–NW33) 71(SW–NW16) 125(SW–NW51)

HEREFORD (Herefs & Worcs). All Saints, late 14th C: 14(SE5) 105(S1E); The Cathedral, early 14th C: 76(SL6E) 101(SL8E) 119(NU7W)

HERNE (Kent). St Martin, early 16th C: 55(S3) 56(N)

LANDBEACH (Cambs). All Souls, mid 14th C?: 129(N2W) 131(S2W)

LAVENHAM (Suffolk). St Peter & St Paul, late 15th C: 44, 59(N1)

LINCOLN (Lincs). The Minster, late 14th C: 1(NL3) 29(RSS5) 104(NU14) 113(SU9) 124(SU5) 143(SU21)

LONDON (South Kensington). Victoria & Albert Museum. ex BLAGDON (Avon), 15th C: 136; ex East Anglia, 15th C: 4, 120; ex KING'S LYNN (Norfolk). St Nicholas, 15th C: Woodcarver in Intro.; (Stepney): The Royal Foundation of St Katherine in Ratcliffe, late 14th C: 110, 126, 151; (Westminster). The Abbey, Henry VII's Chapel, ca 1509: 20(SL6E) 15(NU1E fourth bay) 17(SU1E fourth bay) 146(NU5E second bay); 122(SU5E, second bay) [late 13th C].

LUDLOW (Salop). St Lawrence: 99(N3E) [1389]; 9(S11E) 111(N2E)[1435]

NORWICH (Norfolk). The Cathedral: 140(N13W) [1420]; 66(S24W) 40(S25W) [1480]

OLD MALTON (N. Yorks). St Mary, late 15th/early 16th C: 88(NU2E)

OXFORD (Oxon). All Souls College Chapel,

1442: 84(N16); New College Chapel, late 14th C: Leaning staff in Intro. (S27E) 83(S7E) 117(N15E) 130(N7E)

RIPON (N. Yorks). The Minster, 1489–94: 93(S10W) 141(S15W) 142(S8W), 144 (S14W)

RIPPLE (Herefs & Worcs). St Mary, 15th C: 8, 12

SHERBORNE (Dorset). The Abbey, mid 15th C: 2(S4) 147(S1)

STRATFORD-UPON-AVON (Warwickshire). Holy Trinity, late 15th C: 34(N4) 35(S2) 72(N13) 116(S6) 133 (S3)

WELLS (Somerset). The Cathedral, ca 1330–40: 42 (outside the choir) 62(S6, first row) 67(S4, first row)

WESTON-IN-GORDANO (Somerset). St Peter & St Paul, probably early 14th C: Intro.

WINCHESTER (Hants). The Cathedral, ca 1305: 47, 48(N10W) 78, 79(N25W) 87(S19W) 102, 103(N8W) 123 (N28W); The College Chapel, ca 1390–95: 7(N2W) 50(S5W) 69, 70(N3W) 92(S1W) 112(S4W)

WINDSOR (Berks). St George's Chapel, 1477–83: Intro., 11(SL8EB) 12(SL7WB) 22(RSSU2) 30, 31, 32(RSSU1) 61(NU2) 64(N25U) 65(NLR5EB) 80(SU14) 81(SU5) 90(NU2) 121(SL8WB) 132(SL10WB) 148(SU14) 'supping with Devil' p. 121 (SL5WB)

WORCESTER (Herefs & Worcs). The Cathedral, late 14th C: 21(S9E) 37(N15E) 60(S10E) 89(S3E) 115(N14E) 135(N2E)

LOCATIONS OF OTHER ENGLISH MISERICORDS

Extracted from *A Catalogue of Misericords in Great Britain* by G. L. Remnant.

Aldington, Kent: St Martin
Alton, Hants: St Laurence
Anstey, Herts: St George
Arundel, W. Sussex: The Castle, FitzAlan Chapel
Astley, Warwickshire: St Mary
Attleborough, Norfolk: St Mary
Aylesbury, Bucks: St Mary
Aylsham, Norfolk: St Michael
Bakewell, Derbyshire: All Saints
Balsham, Cambs: Holy Trinity
Bebington, Merseyside: St Andrew
Beddington, Surrey: St Mary the Virgin
Bedford, Beds: St Paul's
Belchamp, Essex: St Paul's
Benefield, Northants: St Mary
Bildeston, Suffolk: St Mary Magdalen
Binham, Norfolk: St Mary
Bishop Auckland, Co Durham: St Andrew
Blackburn, Lancs: St Mary
Blakeney, Norfolk: St Nicholas
Bodmin, Cornwall: St Petroc with St Leon
Bolton-le-Moors, Lancs: St Peter
Bovey Tracy, Devon: St Peter and St Paul
Brampton, Hunts: St Mary Magdalene
Brancepeth, Co Durham: St Brandon
Broadwater, W. Sussex: St Mary
Brundish, Suffolk: St Lawrence
Bury St Edmund's: Moyse's Hall Museum
Cambridge, Cambs: Jesus College; Pembroke College; Peterhouse
Cambridge, Cambs: St Clement's
Canon Pyon, Herefs & Worcs: St Lawrence
Canterbury, Kent: Holy Cross
Castle Acre, Norfolk: St James
Castle Hedingham, Essex: St Nicholas
Caston, Norfolk: The Holy Cross
Cawston, Norfolk: St Agnes
Chichester, W. Sussex: St Mary's Hospital

Church Gresley, Derbyshire: St George and St Mary
Cley, Norfolk: St Margaret
Cliffe-at-Hoo, Kent: St Helen
Clifton Campville, Staffs: St Andrew
Cobham, Kent: St Mary Magdalen
Cockfield, Suffolk: St Peter
Cockington, Devon: St George and St Mary
Coddenham, Suffolk: St Mary the Virgin
Collingham, North, Notts: All Saints
Colton, Staffs: B.V.M.
Coventry, W. Midlands: Henry VIII's Grammar School; Holy Trinity
Darlington, Co Durham: St Cuthbert
Darrington, W. Yorkshire: St Luke and All Saints
Denham, Suffolk: St John the Baptist
Doddington, Great, Northants: St Nicholas
Duntisbourne Rous, Glos: St Michael
Durham, Co Durham: The Castle, Bishop Tunstall's Chapel; The Cathedral
Eccleshall, Staffs: Holy Trinity
Elmham, North, Norfolk: St Mary the Virgin
Enville, Staffs: St Mary
Eversden, Great, Cambs: St Mary
Exeter, Devon: Royal Albert Memorial Museum
Fairford, Glos: St Mary
Fairwell, Staffs: St Bartholomew
Fordham, Cambs: St Peter and St Mary Magdalene
Fornham, Suffolk: St Martin
Framsden, Suffolk: St Mary
Gamlingay, Cambs: St Mary
Garstang, Lancs: St Helen's
Gayton, Northants: St Mary
Godmanchester, Cambs: St Mary the Virgin
Greystoke, Cumbria: St Andrew
Grimston, Norfolk: St Botolph
Hackness, N. Yorks: St Mary the Virgin

Halford, Warwickshire: St Mary
Halifax, W. Yorks: St John
Halsall, Lancs: St Cuthbert
Hardham, W. Sussex: St Botolph
Harling, East, Norfolk: St Peter and St Paul
Hemingbrough, N. Yorks: Blessed Virgin Mary
Hemington, Northants: St Peter and St Paul
Hereford, Herefs & Worcs: St Peter's
Hexham, Northumberland: The Abbey
Higham Ferrers, Northants: St Mary
Highworth, Wilts: St Michael
Holdenby, Northants: All Saints
Holdgate, Salop: Holy Trinity
Holme Lacy, Herefs & Worcs: St Cuthbert
Irthlingborough, Northants: St Peter
Isham, Northants: St Peter
Isleham, Cambs: St Andrew
Kidlington, Oxon: St Mary the Virgin
Kingsbridge, Devon: St Edmund
King's Lynn, Norfolk: St Margaret
Knowle, W. Midlands: St John the Baptist, St Lawrence and St Anne
Lanchester, Co Durham: All Saints
Lavant, East, W. Sussex: St Mary
Ledbury, Herefs & Worcs: St Michael and All Angels
Leighton Buzzard, Beds: All Saints
Leintwardine, Herefs & Worcs: St Mary Magdalene
Lexham, East, Norfolk: St Andrew
Lingfield, Surrey: St Peter and St Paul
Litcham, Norfolk: All Saints
Loversall, W. Yorks: St Katherine
Lynn, West, Norfolk: St Peter
Madley, Herefs & Worcs: St Mary
Maidstone, Kent: All Saints
Malpas, Cheshire: St Oswald
Malvern, Great, Herefs & Worcs: The Priory Church of St Mary and St Michael
Manchester, Gt Manchester: The Cathedral
Marston, North, Bucks: St Mary
Mere, Wilts: St Michael the Archangel
Micheldean, Glos: St Michael
Middleton, Gt Manchester: St Leonard
Middleton by Pickering, N. Yorks: St Andrew
Middlezoy, Somerset: Holy Cross
Milton, Cambs: All Saints
Milton Abbas, Dorset: St James the Great and Other Saints
Minster-in-Thanet, Kent: St Mary
Moccas, Herefs & Worcs: St Michael
Nantwich, Cheshire: St Mary
Newark, Notts: St Mary Magdalen
Northill, Beds: St Mary Virgin
Norton, Suffolk: St Andrew
Norwich, Norfolk: St Gregory; St Margaret; St Mary-at-Coslany; St Peter Mancroft; St Stephen
Nottingham, Notts: St Stephen, Sneinton
Oakley, Great, Northants: St Michael
Occold, Suffolk: St Michael
Orwell, Cambs: St Andrew
Ottery St Mary, Devon: St Mary the Virgin
Oulton, Suffolk: St Michael
Over, Cambs: St Mary
Oxford, Oxon: Christ Church Cathedral; Lincoln College; Magdalen College
Passenham, Northants: St Guthlac
Penkridge, Staffs: St Michael and All Angels
Peterborough, Northants: The Cathedral
Prescot, Merseyside: Our Lady
Ranworth, Norfolk: St Helen
Richmond, N. Yorks: St Mary
Rotherham, S. Yorks: All Saints
Rothwell, Northants: Holy Trinity
St Burian, Cornwall: St Buryan
St German's, Cornwall: St Germanus
St Neots, Cambs: St Mary
Salhouse, Norfolk: All Saints
Salisbury, Wilts: The Cathedral; St Thomas of Canterbury
Salle, Norfolk: St Peter and St Paul
Sandwich, Kent: St Clement's
Screveton, Notts: St Wilfred
Sedgefield, Co Durham: St Edmund
Soham, Cambs: St Andrew
Southwell, Notts: The Minster
Southwold, Suffolk: St Edmund
Sprotborough, S. Yorks: St Mary the Virgin

Staindrop, Co Durham: St Mary
Stamford, Lincs: Browne's Hospital
Stanford, Northants: Holy Trinity with St James the Greater
Stevenage, Herts: St Nicholas with Holy Trinity
Stiffkey, Norfolk: St Mary
Stoke-by-Nayland, Suffolk: St Mary the Virgin
Stowlangtoft, Suffolk: St George
Sudbury, Suffolk: St Gregory; St Peter
Sutton Courtenay, Berks: All Saints
Swinbrook, Oxon: St Mary
Swine, Humberside: St Mary
Swineshead, Beds: St Nicholas
Tansor, Northants: St Mary
Tarring, West, W. Sussex: St Andrew
Tattershall, Lincs: Holy Trinity College Chapel
Tewkesbury, Glos: The Abbey
Thompson, Norfolk: St Martin
Throwley, Kent: St Michael and All Angels
Thurgarton Notts: The Priory Church of St Peter
Tideswell, Derbyshire: St John the Baptist

Tilney, Norfolk: All Saints
Tong, Salop: St Mary with St Bartholomew
Trunch, Norfolk: St Botolph
Ufford, Suffolk: The Assumption
Wakefield, W. Yorks: Cathedral Church of All Saints
Walpole, Norfolk: St Peter
Walsall, Staffs: St Matthew
Walsham, North, Norfolk: St Nicholas
Wantage, Berks: St Peter and St Paul
Wellingborough, Northants: All Saints
Westwell, Kent: St Mary
Wetheringsett, Suffolk: All Saints
Whalley, Lancs: St Mary
Wimborne, Dorset: St Cuthberga
Wingfield, Suffolk: St Andrew
Wingham, Kent: St Peter
Wittering, West, W. Sussex: St Peter and St Paul
Worle, Somerset: St Martin
Wysall, Notts: Holy Trinity
York, N. Yorks: The Minster; All Saints, North Street; St Mary, Castlegate; (St Saviour, but now in care of Clerk of Works, York Minster)

ACKNOWLEDGEMENTS

Far too many friendly and helpful people contributed to this book in various ways for me to acknowledge them individually. They ranged from churchmen all over England, through people entrusted with the keys of porch doors nowadays increasingly locked against vandalism, to volunteer workers in the midst of cleaning up or decorating. All proved unfailingly kind to a camera-laden stranger usually in something of a hurry (most of my misericord photography involved weekend hire-car drives during many brief stays in the United Kingdom on other business) and seeking access to the choir between weddings, funerals and Sunday services. My special thanks are due to the Deans, Masters and Bursars responsible for the College Chapels of Oxford and Cambridge, the Headmaster and Bursar of Winchester College, Mr Clive Wainwright of the Victoria and Albert Museum, and Major General R. L. C. Dixon, CB, MC, Chapter Clerk, Windsor Castle; also to the Vicar of St Martin's Herne, for a stimulating conversation on ducks and herons on a cold December morning in 1981 and Ms Angie Eccles for the Scotch bat on p 121. Invaluable technical advice and assistance were received from Mr A. Schendel of Zeiss/ West Germany and Mr M. Horino, President of Minicam Research Corporation, Tokyo; also from Messrs R. Ficken of The Memorial University of Newfoundland and D. W. Worsnop of Wellsford, New Zealand. Mr Ficken processed all my film over my years of residence in Newfoundland, perfecting the sepia toning procedure that Mr Worsnop had the challenging task of matching for later photographs that I took in 1984.

REFERENCES

1 Anderson, M. D. (also listed under her married name, Cox, T.) 1935. *The Medieval Carver*. Cambridge University Press (CUP).

2 Anderson, M. D. 1954. *Misericords* (King Penguin). Penguin Books, Harmondsworth.

3 Anderson, M. D. 1969. 'The iconography of British misericords', pp. xxiii-xl *in* Remnant, hereunder.

4 Barnard, J. L. (undated reference to his linking of some Westminster Abbey misericord designs with late 15th-century German prints). *in* Bond, 1910b, hereunder.

5 Berners, Dame Juliana 1486. *The Boke of Saint Albans*. Elliot Stock, London. 1905 facsimile.

6 Bond, F. 1910a. *Wood Carvings in English Churches*. I.—Misericords. Oxford University Press (OUP).

7 Bond, F. 1910b. *Wood carvings in English Churches*. II.—Stalls and Tabernacle Work. OUP.

8 Bond, F. 1913. *An Introduction to English Church Architecture*. Vols I & II. OUP.

9 Bond, F. 1914. *Dedications and Patron Saints of English Churches*. OUP.

10 Brusewitz, G. 1969. (Transl. by W. Wheeler from Swedish). *Hunting*. George Allen & Unwin, London.

11 Cave, C. J. P. 1948. *Roof Bosses in Medieval Churches*. CUP.

12 Clarke, K. M. 1920. 'The misericords of Exeter Cathedral', *Devon & Cornwall Notes and Queries 11*, II.

13 Collins, J. K. 1874. *Examples of English Mediaeval Foliage*. Batsford, London.

14 Cox, T. 1959. 'The twelfth-century design sources of the Worcester Cathedral misericords', *Archaeologia 97*, 165–178.

15 Cozens-Hardy, B. 1928. *History of St Margaret's, Cley*.

16 Creighton, C. 1891, 1894. *A History of Epidemics in Britain*. Vols I & II. CUP.

17 Curley, M. J. (transl.) 1979. *Physiologus*. University of Texas Press, Austin & London.

18 Dal, E. & Skårup, P. 1980. *The Ages of Man and the Months of the Year. Hist. Filos. Medd. Dan. Vid. Selsk. 9*.

19 Dent, A. 1974. *Lost Beasts of Britain*. Harrap, London.

20 *Dictionary of National Biography*. 1975. Compact Edition, Vols. I & II. OUP.

21 Ditchfield, P. H. 1896. *Old English Customs*. George Redway, London.

22 Druce, G. C. 1914. 'Animals in English wood carvings', *Walpole Soc. 3*, 57–73.

23 Farley, J. 1981. *The Misericords of Gloucester Cathedral*. Jack Farley, The King's School, Gloucester.

24 Friedman, J. B. 1981. *The Monstrous Races in Medieval Art and Thought*. Harvard University Press.

25 Fussell, G. E. (1952). 1981 reprint. *The Farmer's Tools*. Bloomsbury Books, London.

26 Gardner, A. 1951. *English Medieval Sculpture*. CUP.

27 Gunther, R. T. 1934. *The Greek Herbal of Dioscorides*. Hafner, London & New York. 1968 facsimile.

28 Heseltine, G. C. (compiler). 1931. *The Kalendar & Compost of Shepherds*. (From the original edition of Guy Marchant, Paris, 1493.) Peter Davies, London.

29 Holland, Philemon (transl.). 1601. Pliny's Natural History translated as *The Historie of the World*. Adam Islip, London. 1634, 1635 edition.

30 Howard, F. E. & Crossley, F. H. 1918. *English Church Woodwork*. Batsford, London.

31 Hudson, N. (ed. & introduced by). 1954. *An Early English Version of Hortus Sanitatis* (including a facsimile of *The Noble Lyfe & Natures of Man . . .*, ca 1521, Jan van Doesborgh, Antwerp). Quaritch, London.

32 Jacob, E. F. 1961. *The Fifteenth Century 1399–1485*. Clarendon Press, Oxford.

33 Kelly, Rev. B. (ed.). 1936. *Butler's Lives of the Saints*. Vols. I–VI. Virtue, London, Dublin & Belfast.

34 Klingender, F. (posthumously ed. by E. Antal & J. Harthan). 1971. *Animals in Art and Thought*. Routledge & Kegan Paul, London.

35 Kraus, D., & Kraus, H. 1975. *The Hidden World of Misericords*. Braziller, New York.

36 Lincoln, F. C. 1959. 'Bird banding'. pp. 623–626 in Vol. 3, *Encyclopaedia Britannica*. Chicago, London & Toronto.

37 Long, G. 1932. *Churches With a Story*. Werner Laurie, London.

38 Luard, H. R. (ed.). 1872–1883. *Matthaei Parisiensis chronica majora*. Vols. I-VII. Rolls Series.

39 Maccoll, D. S. 1905. 'Grania in church: or the clever daughter.' *Burlington Mag.* 8, 80–86.

40 Mackie, J. D. (1952) 1966 edition. *The Earlier Tudors 1485–1558*. Clarendon Press, Oxford.

41 Mandeville, Sir John 1484. *The Travels. . . .* Transl. von Diemeringen. Johann Prüss, Strassburg.

42 Markham, V. R. 1929. *Romanesque France*. John Murray, London.

43 Moffett, T. 1655. *Health's Improvement* . . . (late 16th century but publ. posthumously).

44 Morris, P. 1983. *Hedgehogs*. Whittet Books, Weybridge, Surrey.

45 Peterson, R., Mountfort, G. & Hollom, P. A. D. (1954). 1961 edition. *A Field Guide to the Birds of Britain and Europe*. Collins, London.

46 Phipson, E. 1896. *Choir Stalls and their Carvings*. Batsford, London.

47 Purvis, Rev. J. S. 1936. 'The use of continental woodcuts and prints by the "Ripon School" of woodcarvers in the early sixteenth century', *Archaeologia* 85, 107–128.

48 Remnant, G. L. 1969. *A Catalogue of Misericords in Great Britain*. Clarendon Press, Oxford.

49 Rendell, A. W. (transl.) 1928. *Physiologus*. Bumpus, London.

50 Seward, A. C. 1935. 'The foliage, flowers and fruit of Southwell Chapter House,' *Proc. Cambridge Antiquarian Soc.* 35, 1–32.

51 Simson, O. von 1956. *The Gothic Cathedral*. Pantheon, New York (quoting Abbé Bulteau).

52 Speed, J. 1614. *The History of Great Britaine*. Sudbury & Humble, London.

53 Steele, R. (ed.). 1893. *Medieval Lore*. [A digest of Berthelet's (1535) edition of the mid 13th-century *De Proprietatibus Rerum* by Bartholomew Anglicus]. Elliot Stock, London.

54 Toy, Rev. Canon J. 1985. Personal communication, 25 Oct. 1985.

55 Tusser, T. 1580 ed. as *Five Hundred Points of Good Husbandry*. Tregaskis, London. 1931 reprint.

56 Varty, K. 1967. *Reynard the Fox*. Leicester University Press.

57 Wagner, A. R. 1959. 'The swan badge and the swan knight', *Archaeologia* 97, 127–138

58 Wildridge, T. T. 1879. *The Misereres of Beverley Minster*. (Plaxton, Hull). The Moxton Press Ltd, Ben Rhydding, West Yorkshire. 1982 facsimile reprint.

59 Yapp, B. 1981. *Birds in Medieval Manuscripts*. The British Library, London.

60 Zarnecki, G. 1951. *English Romanesque Sculpture 1066–1140*. Alec Tiranti Ltd, London.